# Fostering Improved Staff Performance

"The Best of Exchange"
Reprint Collection #3

A collection of articles
reprinted from past issues of
**Child Care Information Exchange**

**Child Care Information Exchange**
Post Office Box 2890
Redmond, WA 98073
(206) 883-9394

CHILD CARE INFORMATION EXCHANGE
PO Box 2890
Redmond, WA 98073

TELEPHONE: (206) 883-9394

PUBLISHER/EDITOR:
Roger Neugebauer

MANAGING EDITOR:
Bonnie Neugebauer

ADVERTISING REPRESENTATIVE:
Steve MacInnis

PRODUCTION EDITOR:
Sandy Brown

SUBSCRIPTION MANAGER:
Ute Kidder

CUSTOMER SERVICES MANAGER:
Nancy Ryan

CUSTOMER RELATIONS MANAGER:
Ann Warren

RESEARCH ASSOCIATE:
Susan Morris

ISSUE DATES: Bimonthly

SUBSCRIPTIONS: $35/Year (6 issues)
To subscribe, mail your payment to the above address or call in your order with credit card information to (800) 221-2864.

ISBN # 0-942702-10-7

Printed in the United States of America

© Exchange Press Inc., 1991

# Fostering Improved Staff Performance
"The Best of Exchange"
Reprint Collection #3

— Table of Contents —

Page 3 — **Self-Motivation: Motivation at Its Best**
by Roger Neugebauer (October 1984)

Page 8 — **Promoting Harmonious Staff Relationships**
by Clare Cherry (June 1980)

Page 12 — **How to Be an Effective Supervisor**
by Theodore Caplow (January 1986)

Page 17 — **Guidelines for Effective Use of Feedback**
by Roger Neugebauer (July 1983)

Page 21 — **How to Give Constructive Criticism**
by David Viscott, MD (May 1986)

Page 25 — **Helping Employees Cope with Change**
by Lorraine Schrag, Elyssa Nelson, and Tedi Siminowsky (September 1985)

Page 31 — **How to Stimulate Creativity in Your Staff**
by Roger Neugebauer (January 1981)

Page 35 — **The Ten Best Ways to Reward Good Work**
advice from Michael LeBoeuf (July 1986)

Page 39 — **A Reappraisal of Praise**
ideas of Richard E. Farson (September 1981)

Page 41 — **How Did You Manage That? A Closer Look at Staff Guidance**
by Pauline Davey Zeece (July 1991)

Page 46 — **Managing Teacher Performance While Walking Around**
by Kay Albrecht (March 1991)

# Self-Motivation: Motivation at Its Best

## by Roger Neugebauer

The director of Funny Bunny Nursery School was concerned. Incidents of lateness and absenteeism among her teachers were increasing. The teachers had stopped planning activities in advance and showed little enthusiasm in working with the children. They also complained continually about everything from inadequate equipment to low wages.

She decided that what was needed to improve staff performance was to tighten discipline. She required teachers to submit daily lesson plans for her approval. She had them sign in and out and deducted pay for lateness and unexcused absences. She kept a closer watch on the classrooms and reprimanded teachers who were sloughing off.

The results were mixed. Lateness and absenteeism declined, and lesson plans were being developed; but teachers' attitudes became even worse. They complained more and acted as if working in the classroom were a drudgery.

Next the director tried the opposite approach. She sought to cheer the staff up by granting them wage increases, setting up a comfortable teachers' lounge, and holding occasional staff parties.

Once again she was disappointed. Although the staff acted happier and complained less, they still exhibited little enthusiasm in their work with the children.

## The Jackass Fallacy

One reason the director's remedies failed is that she was operating from overly simplistic notions about what motivates people to work hard. She acted as if the teachers were naturally lazy and irresponsible, as if they could only be made to work hard through fear of punishment or promise of rewards. This carrot and stick approach may work perfectly well in motivating a jackass, but it is wholly inappropriate in motivating people. As Harry Levinson, creator of the *Jackass Fallacy* analogy, explains:

"As long as anyone in a leadership role operates with such a reward-punishment attitude toward motivation, he is implicitly assuming that he has control over others and that they are in a jackass position with respect to him. This attitude is inevitably one of condescending contempt whose most blatant mask is paternalism. The result is a continuing battle between those who seek to wield power and those who are subject to it."

## What Does Motivate Teachers?

In 1975, this author interviewed 64 child care teachers about what satisfies them and what frustrates them in their work. In reviewing the major sources of satisfaction (see summary below), it can be seen that they relate directly to the *content* of the teachers' work. These factors—observing progress in children, relationships with children—result directly from the way teachers perform their work. On the other hand, the major sources of frustration—rate of pay, supervision, personnel policies—relate to the *environment* in which the work is performed.

Based on similar findings in studies in a wide variety of professions (see Herzberg), organizational psychologists have reached a number of conclusions on what can be done to motivate workers. When the environmental factors are not adequately provided for (i.e. when pay is low or the environment is oppressive), workers will become frustrated. However, when these factors are adequately provided for, this will usually have no important positive effect—these factors do nothing to elevate an individual's desire to do his job well. The content-related factors, commonly referred to as *motivators*, on the other hand, can stimulate workers to perform well. They provide a genuine sense of satisfaction.

A director seeking to bolster the sagging morale of her teachers, therefore, will have only limited success if she focuses solely on the environmental factors—increasing pay, improving physical arrangements, making supervision less rigid. If the teachers' lounge is renovated, teachers may become less frustrated, but they won't necessarily work harder on the job because of this change. To truly motivate the teachers, a director needs to focus her attention on restructuring the teachers' jobs so that they can derive more satisfaction directly from their work.

## Examining Motivators More Closely

But how does one go about restructuring a teacher's job to take advantage of these motivating factors? Taking a cue from organizational psychologists, a director should strive to meet the following criteria in restructuring a job (Hackman):

**1. Meaningfulness.** A teacher must feel her work is important, valuable, and worthwhile. If a teacher believes her work is unimportant, it won't really matter to her whether or not she does it well. If she believes her teaching does have a significant impact on children's lives, she will work hard to see that the impact is a positive one.

**2. Responsibility.** A teacher must feel personally responsible and accountable for the results of the work he performs. If a teacher is simply carrying out the plans and instructions of a supervisor, he will derive little personal satisfaction when things go well. If he has complete control over the planning and implementation of daily activities in his room, he will know that when children are thriving it is due to his efforts.

**3. Knowledge of results.** A teacher must receive regular feedback on the results of her efforts. If a teacher exerts a major effort on an activity but receives no indication as to whether or not it was successful, she will gain no satisfaction. A teacher can only derive satisfaction from the positive results she knows about.

The remainder of this article will be devoted to describing specific examples of how to apply these criteria.

## Clarifying Goals

Before teachers can be satisfied with the results of their efforts, they must be clear as to what results were expected in the first place. The center must have goals which teachers can use as yardsticks to evaluate their accomplishments. To be effective, a center's goals must:

**1. Be compatible with the personal goals of teachers.** Teachers will work hardest to accomplish organizational goals which are most similar to their own goals. Some centers achieve a close fit between organizational and personal goals by involving the teachers in developing the goals at the beginning of the year. Other organizations accomplish this by holding planning conferences between the director and individual staff members. In these conferences the employee outlines her personal interest and career goals. The two then develop ways in which the individual can work toward the accomplishment of her and the organization's goals at the same time (McGregor). For example, if one of a teacher's goals is to develop her creative movement skills and one of the center's goals is to stimulate children's imaginations, the teacher might be assigned to develop and use movement activities which challenge children's imaginations.

**2. Provide a moderate challenge to teachers.** Experiments have shown that most workers respond best to goals which are moderately difficult to achieve (Gellerman). The goal must not be so ambitious that it cannot possibly be achieved, nor so easy that it can be accomplished with little effort. Such moderately challenging goals should be established for the program as a whole (for example, to double the amount of cooperative play among the children) as well as for individual children (i.e. to help David control his temper).

## Encouraging Self-Control

A key to outgrowing a jackass style of management is shifting control over teachers' performances from the director to the teachers themselves. Ideally, a teacher and a director could agree upon a set of goals for a classroom at the beginning of the year. The teacher would then be fully responsible for planning and implementing daily activities to achieve these goals. At the end of a set time period (the less experienced the staff the more modest the goals and the shorter the time period) the teacher would be held accountable for having accomplished the goals. The teacher would work hard, not because he was being closely watched by the director, but because he was personally committed to achieving the goals.

Centers have developed many ways of supporting teachers in controlling their own performance. One center has the teachers write and periodically revise their job descriptions and the rules for various classroom areas. Another provides teachers with sufficient petty cash so they won't have to keep running to the director to request money to buy routine supplies and equipment. A third has teachers bring problems with children before their peers so that teachers can learn to solve their own problems.

Not all teachers will be willing or able to function so independently. Some will always feel more comfortable having someone else take the lead and issue directions. Other teachers may be ready to accept responsibility, but not for a full classroom. These teachers could have their self-control supported by being assigned full responsibility for a small number of children, for a certain activity area, or for performing a specific function (such as offering support and encouragement to children).

## Providing Feedback

When teachers were asked what satisfies them, they happily cited incidents such as: "When children beam after finally accomplishing a task"; "Seeing examples of children's cooperative play steadily increase"; or "When a parent comments on how a child's behavior is dramatically improving at home thanks to the school."

Given the high motivational impact of incidents such as these, a director should give high priority to seeing to it that they happen as often as possible. To get an idea of how a director might do this, the hundreds of motivating incidents supplied by teachers were analyzed. The majority of these incidents were

---

### Major Sources of Satisfaction and Frustration

In a survey of 64 teachers in 24 New England child care programs, the following were identified as their major sources of satisfaction and frustration in their work. (They are listed in order of frequency.)

Sources of Satisfaction

1. Observing progress in children
2. Relationships with children
3. Challenge of the work
4. Pride in performing a service
5. Relationships with parents
6. Recognition shown by staff

Sources of Frustration

1. Rate of pay
2. Prospects for advancement
3. Physical work environment
4. Style of supervision
5. Number of hours worked
6. Inflexible personnel policies

found to fall into three primary categories which are listed below. With each category, ideas are listed which a director can use to encourage that type of motivation.

**1. Immediate reactions of children to an activity or to accomplishing a task.**

• Help teachers develop their skills in observing children's subtle signs of change or satisfaction.

• Ask teachers to list incidents of children's reactions and changes (pro and con) on a single day or week. This will force them to be alert for such feedback which they may otherwise be too preoccupied to notice.

• Periodically ask parents for incidents of children's progress or follow through on school activities. Pass these on to the children's teachers.

• Recruit volunteers to teach so that teachers can occasionally step back and observe what's going on in the classroom.

• Provide feedback to teachers focusing on effects of teaching on children rather than on the teachers' methods or styles.

• Set aside a time on Fridays when teachers can pause to reflect on what went wrong and what went right during the week. Devote occasional staff meetings to having teachers share their good experiences from the week.

**2. Warm relationships established with the children and their parents.**

• Provide times and places where teachers can have relaxed intimate conversations with individual children.

• Make teachers responsible for a small number of children so they can better get to know each other.

• Before the school year begins, have teachers visit children's homes to establish rapport with the families.

• Encourage families to keep in touch with the center after their children *graduate*.

• Assign each teacher responsibility for maintaining regular communications with specific parents.

• Bring in volunteers at the end or beginning of the day so that teachers can have informal uninterrupted conversations with parents.

**3. Indications of the long-range progress of children.**

• Make teachers responsible for long periods of time for complete units of work. If teachers' responsibilities are continuously shifting from one group of children to another, or from one curriculum area to another, they will never be able to attribute any long-term changes in children primarily to their own efforts.

• Keep diaries of children's behavior so that changes in children can be tracked.

• Videotape classroom activities periodically and compare children's behavior as the year progresses.

• At regular intervals tabulate the number of incidents of specific behaviors which occur in a set time period to determine if there are any changes in these behaviors.

• Conduct tests on the developmental levels of children throughout the year.

• In regular parent conferences, with teachers present, ask parents to discuss changes they have noted in their children's behavior.

## Promoting Staff Development

One of the most important ways a director can help motivate teachers is to provide them with opportunities to improve their skills. The more skilled teachers are, the more likely they are to experience, and be rewarded by, incidents of success. The director should help teachers identify their specific training needs and secure appropriate training resources. These resources may be in the form of reading material, in-house staff training sessions, or outside workshops and courses.

## Encouraging Broader Involvement

Most teachers will tend to feel better about themselves, as well as more excited about their work, if they are involved in their profession outside the classroom. If teachers are involved in the overall management of their center or in children's advocacy efforts in the community, they will get a stronger sense of their efforts being an integral part of a vital profession.

At the center level, teachers' involvement can be broadened by keeping them continually informed on the status of the organization as a whole, by assigning them limited administrative responsibilities, as well as by involving them, wherever feasible, in major center decision-making.

Centers have also experienced positive results from encouraging their teachers to become involved in professional activities outside the center. Such activities might include participating in advocacy coalitions, working for professional organizations (such as NAEYC chapters), or promoting various child care alternatives in the community. Active teacher involvement in these areas will also relieve some pressure on the director to be the agency's representative on every committee and function.

## Motivation—A Final Perspective

The message of this article is that teachers are their own best source of motivation. If a teacher's work is properly structured, she will be motivated by the results of her own labors, not by external rewards and punishments manipulated by someone else. The director's prime concern should therefore be with helping the teacher achieve control over and feedback from her work.

This is not to say, however, that the director need not be concerned with environmental factors such as wages, personnel policies, and physical environment. Highly motivated teachers will be very tolerant of unavoidable inadequacies in these areas.

However, if conditions deteriorate markedly, especially if this appears to be due to the indifference of *management*, teachers' motivation will rapidly be cancelled out by their growing frustration. Therefore, in motivating teachers by concentrating attention on job content, the director should not ignore the teachers' basic needs.

## References and Resources

Gellerman, Saul W. **Motivation and Productivity.** New York: American Management Association, 1963.

Hackman, J. Richard, and J. Lloyd Suttle. **Improving Life at Work.** Santa Monica, CA: Goodyear Publishing Company, 1977.

Herzberg, Frederick. "One More Time: How Do You Motivate Employees?," **Harvard Business Review**, January-February 1968.

Levinson, Harry. "Asinine Attitudes Toward Motivation," **Harvard Business Review**, January-February 1973.

McGregor, Douglas. **The Human Side of Enterprise.** McGraw-Hill Book Company, 1960.

Neugebauer, Roger. **Organizational Analysis of Day Care.** ERIC Document Reproduction Service, PO Box 190, Arlington, VA 22210.

---

*Editor's Note: This is a revised version of an article which originally appeared in the April 1979 issue of* **Exchange**.

# Promoting Harmonious Staff Relationships

### by Clare Cherry

There are two areas which I see as being critical to the success of any child care center—whether it is a very small program or a very large one, whether it is a very structured program or a very open one. First, the center needs to have a solid financial base. Unless a program is adequately funded, it cannot operate properly. However, no amount of funding, no amount of equipment and supplies, and no amount of beautiful space can result in a good program unless there are harmonious relationships among staff members.

If staff members have good relationships with one another and subscribe to your school's educational philosophy, they are going to feel good about their jobs, and their good feelings will naturally be reflected in their work with the children. If there are negative feelings among staff members, these feelings will most likely reach the children. An adult may think:

*Well, I'll go into my classroom now and love these darling children. I'll put on a big smile, and we'll have a wonderful day. I'll forget the fact that I can't stand Ms. Busybody in the next room and that I think my boss is very narrow minded, and that one of these days I'm going to tell them both off. . . . Hello-o-o, goo-ood morning, children.*

She can hide her negative feelings with words, but her nonverbal language will communicate her feelings to the children. She may not even be aware of it, but the way she is tilting her shoulder, arching her back, tightening her fingers, pursing her lips, or twisting her eyebrows indicate to the children that she is in a tense and negative mood.

So whether negative feelings are expressed in conscious or subconscious behaviors, whether they affect teaching subtly or blatantly, they do get in the way of creating a positive learning environment. It is the director's responsibility to foster harmonious relationships among the adults in a center so that the growth and development of the children can go forward naturally.

To create such an environment, the director needs to encourage free expression of feelings, to promote caring and sharing among staff members, and to be genuinely concerned for the personal needs and problems of individual staff members.

## Encouraging Free Expression

I put a lot of effort into encouraging my staff members to be open and honest in expressing feelings to each other and to me. This free expression does not result from my requiring it to happen, but from their learning to trust themselves. I have found that if I can trust myself to be who I am and not put on artificial postures, then I can be open and honest in my dealing with other people.

When individuals do not trust themselves and begin to withhold or disguise their true feelings, all sorts of barriers start to develop in relationships. For example, a teacher may resent the fact that another teacher is careless with the storage of art supplies. If this minor irritation is not communicated to the other teacher, the resentment may fester inside. Pretty soon, several little resentments, each minor by itself, may build up, one against another, until the two individuals involved are no longer clicking when they see each other and neither understands why. If an atmosphere is developed in which such little irritations can be openly expressed, even though they may hurt at the moment, that openness can nip problems in the bud and lead to the development of understanding and more mature relationships.

Since our society in general does not encourage the open expression of feelings, we all need training in this skill. I like to give my staff opportunities to discuss their feelings and to experience how easy it is to work out problems together. We work on this at staff meetings in one way or another. For example, I may start a meeting discussing financial matters, filling out want lists, and going over attendance problems. Then I might suddenly ask those present:

*I want you to try something for me. Put down on paper exactly how you are feeling right this minute. Not how you felt when you came in and not how relieved you're going to feel when the meeting is over and you can go home—but right now!*

Then we each take turns discussing what we wrote down and why. Later, we learn to just express the feeling; we find there is no need to explain among trusted friends.

Sometimes I ask: "What is the happiest thing that happened to each of you this week?" or "What is the most exciting thing that one of your kids did this week?" Or I might ask: "What was the biggest problem for you at school last week? How did you feel about it? What did you do?" Gradually we all become more aware of the potential of being able to express feelings openly, and we become more sensitive to the feelings of others. This means, of course, that we become more sensitive to the feelings of the children in our care and to the feelings of their parents.

The one thing I absolutely discourage is malicious and petty gossip. I think gossip is an insidious force in any kind of group. Gossip cannot be small because gossip breeds gossip. Gossip implies a lack of respect for another person's uniqueness, thinking, and inner self.

When I hire a new staff person, I say:

*If you come late, I'll be angry. If you take advantage of sick leave, I'll be angry. If your room gets too messy or chaotic, I may well get upset. But I won't fire you.*

*However, if I'm aware that you are involved in gossiping about other staff members, student teachers, or parents, you simply will not work here any more. I know it's hard to avoid indulging in small gossip when you're socializing with others, but the best thing is just to steer clear of it. If something about a teacher upsets you, tell that person.*

I have been critically advised more than once that my expectations are unrealistic and impractical. Well, I certainly don't want people going around hurting and insulting each other.

But I would rather have concerns brought directly to the person involved and be able to trust that person's ability as a dedicated and skilled teacher to handle constructive criticism than to have concerns passed along to others behind the person's back. If it isn't constructive, it shouldn't be said at all.

## Promoting Caring and Sharing

At the first staff meeting each new school year I like to throw out a challenge to all staff members. I challenge each one to see to it that each of the other teachers has the best year teaching they've ever had. The teachers have really responded to this challenge. It used to be that some teachers would horde their ideas behind closed doors so they could really shine in the eyes of the parents and the director. Now they get excited about running around and sharing new ideas, resources, and materials. When one teacher is having a problem with a particular child or parent, the others are eager to offer support and suggestions.

We strive to foster an atmosphere in which each staff member is concerned with the successes and failures of the others. The stage is actually set by the director when she hires new staff members. Each person is carefully evaluated, not only as to personality, education, experience, and other qualifications, but also as to how that person's temperament will blend with the other staff members' temperaments which are already working harmoniously. The goal is not to try to hire people who are all alike but to hire people who are capable of finding compatibility amongst themselves.

Human nature being what it is, not all persons relate well all the time. Occasionally conflicts will develop between two staff members. There are a variety of ways a director can try to resolve such conflicts—giving a pep talk on the importance of positive relations or getting actively involved as a mediator of the conflict. A very simple process to help soften the feelings between two people is to try to get them involved in some task involving the use of their hands—such as realigning all the art supplies, sorting the paper shelf, making sandwiches for a school outing, or making name tags for a parent event.

I think there's a very close relationship between using our hands and verbalization. Somehow people working side by side on such tasks will inevitably start talking with each other—first carefully and then gradually building up to a free flow of thoughts. Tensions that were there begin to break down, sometimes making a complete turnabout so that the two suddenly become good friends. What usually happens is that they find out they have a lot more in common than they have in difference. Knowing this makes the differences more tolerable.

## Showing Concern for Individuals

Teachers' performances will not only be affected by the tone of interpersonal relationships at the center but also by personal problems they may be experiencing outside the center. The director must be like a seismograph—very sensitive to developing problems and tensions. The behavior of teachers in the center may be affected by marital problems, financial difficulties, poor health, or even crises with their own children.

When you sense that the performance of a teacher is being adversely affected by such a crisis, you can respond in a variety of ways. To begin with, it is important to give the troubled staff member an opportunity to discuss the problem. It should be made clear that you are not trying to pry into the teacher's private life; but since the problem is apparently affecting the teacher's professional performance, you would like to offer to help if possible. Sometimes being available to listen, giving the teacher a point of release, is all a director will be able to do or will even need to do.

In other cases, the person may simply need some time off. Maybe you could fill in for the teacher for the remainder of the day or find a substitute for two or three days. Possibly the teacher simply needs to be alone for a short while. Since our school is in a large church building, of which we use only a small part, we have been able to create a few private places where staff members can go and know that their privacy will be respected.

When a personal crisis has greatly affected performance, a director may need to suggest an extended leave of absence. However, such a suggestion should be treated carefully. If the leave is recommended in order to give the person time to work out a personal problem (such as in the case of one of my staff persons whose home was flooded in the severe California storms a few winters ago), the offer is valid. If it is given with the hope that a person's attitudes, emotional responses, or personality will change, the offer is a mistake. To expect people to become something they are not is unrealistic.

The director must accept people as they are and help them make the fullest use of their natural abilities and inner self while at the same time helping them to relegate their problems and handicaps to unimportant roles. If the impact of a person's personal problems on his work cannot be minimized in the foreseeable future, it may be more realistic to consider a termination rather than a leave of absence.

The director can be most supportive of teachers with personal problems by developing individual, personal relationships with all staff members on a regular basis, not just when a crisis develops. To have a regular nonschool communication session with every staff member (19 of them) is not an easy task in our complex lives today. But it's important enough to work on.

I may go out to lunch with individuals; or if scheduling is a real problem, we may meet at school during a break. A touch on the shoulder in the hall and a few moments of "How are things today?" kind of conversation or even a telephone conversation occasionally can help develop a relationship.

No matter what the setting, I try to steer the conversation away from job-related issues. These conversations help communicate to staff members that I care about them as individuals as well as employees and that I am available for listening or whatever else is their need at all times. That's what I like to think I'm being paid for.

Such a caring attitude helps foster a caring and sharing relationship among all the adults in the school community. It enables me to be able to proudly express my own feelings, in all honesty, and say: "My staff is the greatest!"

---

*Clare Cherry, MA, humanistic and transpersonal psychology, has been director of Congregation Emanu El Nursery School and Ungraded Primary in San Bernadino, California, for over 30 years. She is also the director of Catec, an early childhood education consulting firm and an instructor at California State College, San Bernadino. She is the author of* **Think of Something Quiet: Serenity in the Early Childhood Classroom** *(Pitman-Learning Corporation, 1980).*

# How to Be an Effective Supervisor

## by Theodore Caplow

Every human organization can be described as if it were a machine. It is designed for a particular purpose and composed of specialized moving parts. It absorbs energy and materials and converts them into other forms. It requires both routine maintenance and emergency repairs. From time to time some critical part breaks down and the organization ceases to function until the broken part is repaired or replaced.

In some other ways, an organization is spectacularly unlike a machine. Its specialized moving parts—people—are incapable of behaving in a fully mechanical way even on an assembly line or in a marching band. The human parts of an organization never do exactly what the organization wants them to do. Each of them has purposes of his/her own that are incongruent with those of the organization, and each of them participates in the organizational program in an intermittent and individual way.

The subgroups that compose an organization are similarly unreliable. They, too, have goals that are inconsistent with those of the whole organization. Nearly every department and section, for example, seeks to enhance its own importance, even when that involves a loss of efficiency or effectiveness for the whole organization.

**The Organization as a Quasi-Machine**

To put it as plainly as possible, the human organization, as a quasi-machine, seldom runs as smoothly as a real machine in good working order. At any given time some of the quasi-machine's parts are practicing what Thorstein Veblen called "the conscientious withdrawal of efficiency," and other parts are engaged in sabotage, an old French word that originally meant trampling on the product of one's labor with wooden shoes.

On the other hand, no real machine is as effective as a quasi-machine for the accomplishment of tasks under changing conditions. Being human, the quasi-machine can restructure itself as it goes along. The individual parts of which it is composed develop new functions on their own initiative. The interaction between them may lead to coordinated efforts of great subtlety and power.

The operator of a quasi-machine has two recurrent problems—how to keep the thing from falling apart and how to get more work out of it than it is supposedly capable of. What you do to solve these problems is called supervision in some organizations and leadership in others—the latter term being generally preferred in organizations that cannot be certain of achieving their goals, such as armies and orchestras.

Because of that uncertainty and the excitement it produces, a great deal of attention is concentrated on the individual at the top, who, regardless of personal characteristics, assumes, if successful, the charisma that seems to separate leadership from mere supervision. "I have observed," writes David Ogilvy, "that no creative organization, whether it is a research laboratory, a magazine, a Paris kitchen, or an advertising agency, will produce a great body of work unless it is led by a *formidable* individual" (Ogilvy, p. 202). But formidable or not, a charismatic leader, like any other responsible manager, gets the work out by supervising people.

## Principles of Supervision

1. **Set unmistakable goals.** The first step in getting any kind of work done under direct supervision is to make clear what the work is for, why it needs to be done in a particular way, and what constitutes success in its performance. Even in the most elementary collective tasks, it is rash to assume that either the purposes of the task or the desired standards of performance are too obvious to require explanation. In almost every successful performance of a group task, goals and standards must be set in advance, clearly communicated, kept constantly in view, and dramatized along the way.

Goal setting is easiest in elite organizations—the great research laboratory, the three-star restaurant kitchen, the world-renowned orchestra, the champion athletic team—where maximum excellence is sought and everyone expects the leader to demand infinite pains for the sake of excellence. Goal setting is more difficult in mediocre organizations, and it is often useful to concentrate on one aspect of the work for the sake of overall improvement.

I knew a man who ran the typing pool in a large engineering firm and supervised a dozen typists who turned out endless pages of reports and specifications. One day he was moved by the sight of several typists using their erasers at the same time to announce that from then on he would demand perfect, error-free typing. Corrections and erasures would no longer be permitted. Erasers were to be thrown away. The typist who made a mistake of any kind was to discard that page and start again. The first few days of the new system were marked by tears, protests, and a great waste of paper. Thereafter, the error rate declined to a negligible level and stayed there as long as the supervisor remained in charge and was able to explain to each new recruit that the goal was perfect, error-free typing.

2. **Supervise the work more than the worker.** The essence of supervised work is that whatever the worker produces comes to the attention of the supervisor so that every improvement or deterioration in the quality of work (or in the quality of supervision) is noticed and stimulates appropriate feedback. The chef who sits at the kitchen door and tastes every dish as it passes, the office manager who scans every typed page before it goes out, the farmer who looks at the new bales of hay and counts them and checks over the mowing machine and the baler at the end of the day all find it easy to communicate with their workers.

Supervising the worker is another matter entirely. The unnecessary exercise of personal authority is a kind of sabotage endlessly practice by incompetent supervisors. Most people need a zone of freedom around them in order to work well. It is hard to find anyone, no matter how meek or discouraged, who willingly submits to tighter control than the necessities of the work require.

3. **Distinguish between essential and nonessential rules.** There is an old textbook distinction in sociology between *folkways*, which are social practices, and *mores*, which are the rules that hold a society together. Every work group has its own folkways and mores, and the

supervisor is responsible for keeping them distinct.

If you are clear in your own mind about which rules are essential and which are not, you are not likely to fritter away your authority in efforts to get perfect compliance with rules such as "No Smoking" or "All tools must be returned to the tool crib by the end of the day." (If for some special reason it is essential to repress smoking or get all tools returned to the tool crib, the problem must be approached less authoritatively—for example, by calling all those concerned together to develop an enforcement plan.)

But with respect to those few norms that express the organization's moral commitments and do call for perfect compliance, the supervisor's best course is to treat every violation as harshly as his powers allow. Ogilvy provides this edifying example from his experience in the kitchen of a great French restaurant:

"Soon after I joined M. Pitard's brigade, I was faced with a problem of morality for which neither my father nor my schoolmasters had prepared me. The *chef garde-manger* sent me to the *chef saucier* with some raw sweetbreads which smelled so putrid that I knew they would endanger the life of any client who ate them; the sauce would mask their condition, and the client would eat them. I protested to the *chef garde-manger*, but he told me to carry out his order; he knew that he would be in hot water if M. Pitard discovered that he had run out of fresh sweetbreads. What was I to do? I had been brought up to believe that it was dishonorable to inform. But I did just that. I took the putrid sweetbreads to M. Pitard and invited him to smell them. He did so and, without a word to me, went over to the *chef garde-manger* and fired him on the spot. This poor bastard had to leave, then and there." (Ogilvy, p. 203)

4. **Reward sparingly; punish much more sparingly.** The usual form of reward in work groups is praise. The usual form of punishment is criticism. Public praise or public criticism have much higher intensity, of course, than praise or criticism in private. Other forms of reward and punishment are raises and pay reductions, bonuses and fines, promotions and demotions, and the extension and withdrawal of privileges.

It can usually be observed in an organized group that the aversion to a given punishment is greater than the desire for an equivalent reward. This can be demonstrated with laboratory precision by anyone who controls a payroll. Step 1: Raise everybody's wages by 10%. The effect on productivity and morale will be nearly imperceptible. Step 2: After an interval of weeks or months, lower the same wages by 5%. The effect on productivity and morale will be disastrous.

All sorts of variations on this unwise experiment can be devised. For example, raising the wages of part of a work group can be counted on to demoralize those who are not raised. A reduction of pay or privileges amounts to a reduction in the ability of the workers to obtain satisfaction through the organization and, inasmuch as they prefer satisfaction to frustration, they are bound to resist.

But individuals in organized groups seldom evaluate their pay and privileges in absolute terms; they are much more likely to measure what they received by comparison with what others receive. Hence, to bestow a reward on one worker is often to impose a punishment of his peers. Even casual praise may have this unintended effect.

The unintended effects of punishments are even more severe than the backlash of rewards. A punishment, if effective, undermines the position of the victim in his work group and thereby reduces his capacity for effective cooperation. It may also reduce the status of friends and peers, with remote and harmful repercussions.

The foregoing observations are not meant to suggest that rewards and punishments should be withheld, only that they must always be administered with great caution. Praise and criticism ought usually to be private rather than public and understated rather than overstated. Major rewards ought to be reserved for those whose right to them is universally recognized. Major punishments, as a general rule, should not be imposed on persons who are still potentially useful to the organization.

The foregoing warnings do not apply to rewards and punishments that are thoroughly routinized. By all means compliment the pastry chef on his chocolate eclairs if the quality of his work is such that you will surely be able to praise his deep-dish apple pie tomorrow and his brioches the day after.

5. **Give credit where credit is due.** This principle looks simple, but to apply it correctly you need a rather complicated formula for allotting credit and blame, which goes as follows:

*Success should be credited to the entire work group or divided between the entire group and one or several of its members. Failure should be blamed on the supervisor alone or on the manager and the entire group jointly.*

The rationale for this formula is that the manager, having set out to elicit a collective effort from a group, should in fairness credit the group as a whole if that effort is successful. You may in addition acknowledge the special contributions of individuals, but you should not claim any credit yourself for the group's collective effort.

If the collective effort is not forthcoming, you must accept responsibility for having been unable to call it forth since that was your primary task. You may or may not implicate the group as a whole in the failure, but you cannot blame individual members of the group without assigning them responsibility for the collective effort and abdicating your own responsibility.

6. **Listen to complaints sympathetically; never complain in turn.** A little reflection will show you that this follows automatically from the previous principle.

7. **Defend the faith.** The manager of an organization, as we have seen, is the custodian of its sacred symbols and the keeper of its moral character. This means that the supervisor must take the group and its work more seriously than anyone else and know how to assume a ceremonial stance for great occasions. You may be cynical and worldly wise about anything else you please, provided you show an innocent and trusting faith in the value of the collective activity that you supervise. If you lack that faith, and cannot simulate it, you might as well give up and go into some other line of work.

8. **Develop an inner circle.** From the manager's standpoint, an inner circle of lieutenants provides additional eyes, ears, and hands to do his supervising. From the rank-and-file standpoint, the interposition of an intermediary who is partly a supervisor and partly a colleague makes it easier and safer to express complaints, suggestions, and requests. Traditional work groups almost always have an inner circle.

But a circle ought to have at least three members. *"Tres faciunt collegium,"* said a maxim of Roman law—which roughly translated means it takes three to make an inner circle. If the group is too small to support an inner circle of three, the supervisor had better consider doing the job alone. A single lieutenant, or even two, may be more hindrance than help.

9. **Protect the status of subordinates.** Even a small work group without a formal hierarchy does not contain an undifferentiated rank and file. There are significant differences in seniority, technical qualifications, and authority within any group. Although it is not always immediately apparent, all of these statuses are part of the same structure from which the supervisor derives authority. So, unless you respect the prerogatives of your subordinates and insist that others respect them also, you undermine yourself.

10. **Retain final control.** If, as a supervisor, you develop an inner circle of lieutenants and protect their prerogatives long enough, you may discover one day that you are no longer able to get anything done on your own. To avoid that, you need to retain an unshared right to approve (or veto) expenditures and personnel actions. You do not need to initiate them; you *do* need more than token control of them. Unless you have enough power to make independent decisions about financial and personnel matters, you do not have enough power for effective supervision. It may even be wise to act capriciously now and then in order to demonstrate your ability to do so.

11. **Innovate democratically.** Even the most traditional organizations require a surprisingly high rate of innovation to stay in touch with technological and environmental changes. In many cases, the introduction of innovations is the principal part of a supervisor's job, but innovation is hazardous. There are many ways of coming to grief while innovating, and some of the practices that otherwise contribute to effective supervision don't work here.

The effects of an innovation are always somewhat unpredictable. In default of omniscience, the supervisor needs to obtain as much information as possible from all the people who will be affected by the innovation and who have facts or insights about its possible consequences. Because any innovation in an organization affects some people adversely, or seems to, some resistance must be anticipated and the possibility of sabotage is never remote. Thus every innovation, however trivial, needs as much support as can conveniently be mustered.

As both field and laboratory experiments have shown, the way to muster support for an innovation is to bring all the people affected into the planning at an early stage and give them a voice in the decisions that need to be made from the first to the last stages. Successful innovations are discussed, designed, and implemented in an atmosphere of participatory democracy. This may be difficult in an otherwise authoritarian organization, but it is always worth the trouble.

12. **Take infinite pains.** This is the most important principle of direct supervision and the most essential to learn. Some people seem to come by it naturally; others acquire the habit by experience and practice. Inborn or learned, it is what distinguishes genius from mere competence and the great leader from a mediocre one.

The inimitable M. Pitard stationed himself at the waiters' counter and inspected each dish before it left the kitchen. Some dishes he sent back to the kitchen for more work. Similarly, Paul Strand—doing a documentary film about a Malay fishing village—postponed the completion of the final scene for a month because one fisherman got a haircut. He was unwilling to go on with the scene until the fisherman's hair was the same length as it had been when the beginning of the scene was filmed.

## Reference

Ogilvy, David M. "The Creative Chef," in G. A. Steiner, ed., **The Creative Organization**. Chicago: University of Chicago Press, 1965.

*Reprinted with permission from Theodore Caplow's book,* ***Managing an Organization***, *Second Edition (New York: Holt, Rinehart and Winston, 1983).*

*Theodore Caplow is commonwealth professor of sociology at the University of Virginia.*

# Guidelines for Effective Use of Feedback

## by Roger Neugebauer

One of the most critical challenges facing a child care director is improving staff performance. A variety of tools are available to help a director meet this challenge—in-house training, annual appraisals, workshops, conferences, college classes, training films, etc. One of the least glamorous of these tools—providing feedback—is, in fact, the most effective.

With proper feedback, teachers can better control and improve their own performance; without proper feedback, teachers operate blindly, not knowing when their efforts succeed or fail. According to George F. J. Lehner, "... feedback helps to make us more aware of what we do and how we do it, thus increasing our ability to modify and change our behavior..." (Lehner).

Just how blindly teachers operate without feedback was demonstrated in a study at the University of Michigan (McFadden). Twenty preschool teachers were interviewed about their teaching philosophies and methods. They all expressed attitudes favoring a nonauthoritarian, nondirective approach by the teacher. They preferred to show verbal concern and approval rather than disapproval. This was how they described their teaching. Yet, when they were actually observed in the classroom, their behavior was quite different. Observers found their classrooms to be predominantly teacher controlled and teacher centered. Their statements to children characterizing support, approval or encouragement were fewer than ten percent of their total statements (Schwertfeger). Without feedback teachers may well be operating with false assumptions about the nature of their behavior and its effect on children and parents.

But as anyone who has tried to give advice to a teacher about her teaching style well knows, being effective at giving feedback is not an easy task. The natural tendency is for teachers to become defensive when feedback about their performance is presented. This reaction occurs when the receiver perceives a threat to her position in the organization, to her standing in the group, or to her own self-image.

When individuals become defensive, they are unlikely to accept, or even hear, feedback that is being offered. Instead of focusing on the message, a person reacting defensively ". . . thinks about how he appears to others; how he may be seen more favorably; how he may win, dominate, impress, or escape punishment; and/or how he may avoid or mitigate a perceived or an anticipated attack" (Gibb).

Defensiveness is increased when the receiver perceives feedback to be critical. As Douglas McGregor observes, "The superior usually finds that the effectiveness of the communication is inversely related to the subordinates' need to hear it. The more serious the criticism, the less likely is the subordinate to accept it" (McGregor).

Since teachers need feedback to improve their performance, it is important that a director become skilled at giving feedback that is helpful in a way that does not arouse their defensiveness. The following are recommendations on giving effective feedback:

• **Feedback should focus on behavior, not the person.** In giving feedback, it is important to focus on what a person does rather than on what the person is. For example, you should say to a teacher "You talked considerably during the staff meeting" rather than "You're a loudmouth." According to George F. J. Lehner, "When we talk in terms of 'personality traits' it implies inherited constant qualities difficult, if not impossible, to change. Focusing on behavior implies that it is something related to a specific situation that might be changed" (Lehner). It is less threatening to a teacher to hear comments about her behavior than about her traits.

• **Feedback should focus on observations, not inferences.** Observations are what we can see or hear in the behavior of another person. Inferences are interpretations we make based on what we hear or see (Lehner). Inferences are influenced by the observer's frame of references and attitudes. As such they are much less likely to be accurate and to be acceptable to the person observed. Inferences are much more likely to cause defensiveness.

• **Feedback should focus on descriptions, not judgments.** In describing an event a director reports an event to a teacher exactly as it occurred. A judgment of this event, however, refers to an evaluation in terms of good or bad, right or wrong, nice or not nice. Feedback which appears evaluative increases defensiveness (Gibb).

It can readily be seen how teachers react defensively to judgments which are negative or critical. But it is often believed that positive judgments—praise—can be very effective as a motivational and learning tool. However, studies have shown that the use of praise has little long-term impact on employees' performance (Baehler). Often praise arouses defensiveness rather than dispelling it. Parents, teachers and supervisors so often "sugarcoat" criticism with praise ("You had a great lesson today, but. . . .") that "when we are praised, we automatically get ready for the shock, for the reproof" (Farson).

• **Feedback should be given unfiltered.** There is a tendency for a director to sort through all the observations she makes of a teacher, and all the comments she receives about a teacher, and to pass along that information that she, the director, judges to be important or helpful. This filtering of feedback may diminish its value to the teacher. According to Peter F. Drucker, "People can control and correct performance if given the information, even if neither they nor the supplier of information truly understand what has to be done or how" (Drucker).

• **Feedback should be given in small doses.** George F. J. Lehner has observed that "to overload a person with feedback is to reduce the possibility that he may use what he receives effectively" (Lehner). Accumulating observations and comments to share with a teacher in periodic large doses may be efficient for the director in terms of time management, but it may make the feedback too voluminous for the teacher to deal with effectively.

• **Feedback should be given on a timely basis.** If a teacher is given feedback about an incident in her classroom on the day that it occurs, she is much more likely to benefit from this feedback than if it is given to her days or weeks later. When feedback is given close to an event, the recipient is likely to remember all aspects of the event clearly, and thus is able to fit the feedback into a complete picture. When feedback is far removed from the event, the event will be less well remembered and the feedback will make less sense.

An extreme, but not a typical, example of untimely feedback is the annual appraisal. An annual appraisal is an effort to give feedback about performance over the past 365 days. Not only does this concentrated dose of feedback cause information overload, it also is offered at a time removed from the behavior itself. As such it "is not a particularly effective stimulus to learning" (McGregor). Studies have shown that to be effective, performance appraisals "should be conducted not annually, but on a day-to-day basis" (Levinson).

• **Feedback should be given to the teacher as his tool to control his own performance.** A teacher is much more likely to benefit from feedback if it is given without strings attached, to use as he sees fit. If a director provides feedback ("The children were restless during circle time today") and then offers advice on how to use it ("I think you should have it earlier in the day"), the teacher is very likely to react defensively over this effort to control his behavior. "The real strength of feedback," according to Drucker, "is clearly that the information is the tool of the worker for measuring and directing himself."

• **Avoid giving mixed messages.** Through their bodies, eyes, faces, postures and senses people can communicate a variety of positive or negative attitudes, feelings and opinions. While providing verbal feedback to a teacher, a director can communicate a conflicting message with her body language. For example, when verbally communicating a nonjudgmental description of a playground scene, a director may be telecasting very disapproving signals to the teacher with the tension in her voice or the expression on her face.

When presented with such mixed messages, a teacher invariably elects to accept the nonverbal message as the director's true meaning. As a result feedback gets distorted, and an atmosphere of distrust is created. "Right or wrong, the employee feels that you are purposely hiding something or that you are being less than candid." (Hunsaker).

To avoid communicating mixed messages, you should not give feedback when you are angry, upset or excited. Wait until you cool down, so that you can keep your emotions under control as you talk. Also you should develop the habit of monitoring your voice tone, facial expressions and body language whenever you give feedback. Being aware of your body language can help you keep it consistent with your verbal language (Needell).

• **Check for reactions.** Just as you give feedback, the recipient signals her reaction to it with her body language. You should tune in to these signals as you talk. As Phillip Hunsaker recommends, "Constantly be on the lookout for nonverbal signals that indicate that your line of approach is causing your employees to become uncomfortable and lose interest. When this happens, change your approach and your message accordingly" (Hunsaker).

• **Be open to feedback yourself.** To develop an effective working relationship, you need feedback from your employees on their reactions to your behavior as much as they need feedback from you. According to organizational psychologist Harry Levinson, "In a superior-subordinate relationship, both parties influence each other, and both have a responsibility for the task."

In order to accomplish this task, they must be able to talk freely to each other, and each must have the sense of modifying the other. "Specifically, the subordinate must be permitted to express his feelings about what the superior is doing in the relationship and what the subordinate would like him to do to further the accomplishment of the task" (Levinson).

• **Encourage a team approach to feedback.** As director, you have a myriad of important tasks in addition to upgrading staff performance. Therefore, it is not possible for you to free up enough time to provide staff members all the feedback they need to improve their performance. In order to provide an ongoing flow of feedback information, you need to enlist all staff members to be feedback givers to each other.

First, you must create an atmosphere in your center that encourages staff members to accept responsibility for helping each other improve.

Second, you need to train staff members on the proper ways to give feedback. Feedback given in a judgmental, personal or untimely fashion can be devastating and can poison interpersonal relations. Training can take the form of reviewing the guidelines discussed above in a staff meeting, by doing some role-playing, and by having staff members give each other feedback on how they give feedback.

Most of all staff members can learn to be effective feedback givers if you serve as a good model in the way you give feedback.

## References

Baehler, James R. **The New Manager's Guide to Success.** New York: Praeger Publishers.

Drucker, Peter F. **Management: Tasks, Responsibilities, Practices.** New York: Harper and Row, Publishers, 1974.

Farson, Richard E. "Praise Reappraised," **Harvard Business Review**, September-October 1963.

Gibb, Jack R. "Defensive Communications," in David A. Kolb (ed.), **Organizational Psychology: A Book of Readings.** Englewood Cliffs, N.J.: Prentice-Hall, Inc., 1971.

Hunsaker, Phillip L., and Anthony J. Alessandra. **The Art of Managing People.** Englewood Cliffs, N.J.: Prentice-Hall, Inc., 1980.

Lehner, George F. J. "Aids for Giving and Receiving Feedback," **Child Care Information Exchange,** June 1978.

Levinson, Harry. **The Exceptional Executive.** Cambridge: Harvard University Press.

McGregor, Douglas. **The Human Side of Enterprise.** New York: McGraw-Hill Book Company, 1960.

Needell, Cheryl K. "Learning to Level with Employees," **Supervisory Management,** January 1983.

Schwertfeger, Jane. "Issues in Cooperative Training," in Dennis N. McFadden (ed.), **Planning for Action.** Washington, DC: NAEYC, 1972.

# How to Give Constructive Criticism

### by David Viscott, MD

It is often more difficult to give criticism than receive it. People are naturally inhibited about telling other people what is wrong with their work. They don't want to hurt others' feelings and are afraid of being rejected when they point out a truth others may be unwilling to face. When giving criticism in business is seen as offering instruction or explanation, it usually presents little difficulty; but sometimes it can be even more problematic than in a personal relationship. Because business criticism is prompted by necessity, it is often neglected until severe problems develop and is then given abruptly and under stressful circumstances, so that it is equated with failure.

To prevent this, supervisors should try to keep an objective distance, so that they can be effective and yet stay in contact. However, business settings are not spontaneous and there is a tendency to withhold criticism along with other feelings. Instead of pointing out errors as soon as they are noticed, even experienced supervisors tend to wait until they have enough data to warrant risking a confrontation. As a result, they may wait too long, allowing workers to get into more serious trouble before they comment. As difficulties grow, workers feel more self-conscious about their mistakes and are likely to be increasingly defensive about hearing corrections.

The scene is set for conflict.

When a supervisor withholds criticism, he experiences discomfort and irritation. These feelings build, raising the risk of overreaction when the opportunity to criticize finally presents itself. At such times problems can be blown out of proportion and sometimes the wrong person becomes the target of the withheld criticism. Giving criticism improperly has remarkable power to create an atmosphere of alienation, resentment, and inefficiency.

If you have kept communication open by taking every opportunity to praise the good work you see, you shouldn't have any problem in pointing out shortcomings when they arise. Criticism and praise have to go hand in hand. If you only talk about mistakes, the people you supervise will expect to suffer a blow to their self-esteem whenever they see you approach. They will hide or be defended and you'll have difficulty being heard, no matter how good your advice.

The first rule is to make your criticism an extension of some praise. Although it's a good idea to reinforce good work as it happens, negative behavior is more likely to get your attention. The basic reason for criticism is to see the squeaky wheel gets the oil. We focus on weaknesses, not because we are negative, but because pain is our greatest teacher. We are designed by nature to pay attention to danger and to take action to protect ourselves.

When things go well, everyone is pleased to take credit for doing their share, but when there is a problem, people look to hide their deficiencies and deny their role in the downturn. Although people know they have room for improvement, they publicly deny their weaknesses, while secretly dwelling on their shortcomings as they question their competence and fear discovery. In the absence of openness, people blame others and search for a scapegoat. It is important in approaching the squeaky wheels in business that you are aware of this. Oil the squeaky wheel, but examine and adjust the others as well.

Your goal in offering correction is to create a more open work atmosphere in which criticism and praise flow along as part of the work, where people do not dread being singled out, but expect and are pleased to receive attention and instruction when they need it. The following guidelines should help you to give constructive criticism.

## Have Clear Objectives

Before you criticize someone, know what you want to accomplish. At the top of your list should be establishing better, more open communication. You probably won't be able to make all the suggestions or corrections you want, but if you can open the channel between you and the other person, you have opened up the process of working out the problem together. If you don't establish this open relationship, it will continue to remain your biggest obstacle.

If you begin to criticize without knowing what you want to achieve, you are asking for trouble. You risk precipitating a blowup. Keep in mind that having a lot of criticisms to make reflects a closed relationship, one in which negative feelings have been building inside both parties. So be diplomatic and deliberate. You are really opening up your relationship to a greater depth of honesty. This has long been neglected, so be slow and gentle. Pick the time and place.

You want to be heard. You need to get through. So don't set up a situation that is designed to work against you. Avoid meeting with someone just before quitting time when he is already anxious to leave. This will add to his discomfort. Avoid meeting before meal breaks. People get grumpy when they are hungry and their stress tolerance drops.

Pick a place that is private, convenient, and friendly. You want the other person to hear you and put your comments into action. Put yourself in the other person's place. Consider the effect of making your comments in the setting you have chosen. Harsh public criticism alienates everyone and creates a closed, mistrusting atmosphere. When a fellow employee is treated unfairly, it threatens other workers. Embarrassing or humiliating others always works against you. First of all, it is a cruel, punitive act and an abuse of power. It will be seen as heavy handed and unfair even if the criticism is justified.

## Be Positive

Because everyone has some dread of being discovered, it's best to begin by establishing and reinforcing the positive ties between you. People are less able to pay attention when they are afraid. Expressing your appreciation for their efforts reduces anxiety and thus lowers defenses.

View the problem as an entity in its own right. Talk about the problem with distance and encourage the other person to comment on it from the same perspective. The object is to acknowledge that a problem exists and establish a way of talking about it that produces results rather than increases conflict.

If the other person doesn't admit that there is a problem, present your evidence simply and without emotion. If you've been withholding criticism for a while, this is the moment when you run the greatest risk of losing control. The older your complaints, the less immediate and believable your criticism will sound. The other person will have poorer memory for distant events and will be less willing to concede your points, and may even resent you for bringing up old issues.

This is a good time to restate your original goals to see if you both share the same understanding. Explain that you want to review the problem from the beginning and that you didn't comment earlier because you believed the problem would clear up. Admit that your judgment was wrong because the problem has persisted.

Accept some of the blame for the problem. This creates a feeling of mutual concern. Perhaps you were misunderstood. Perhaps you did not express yourself clearly or failed to make sure that the other person really understood you. Maybe the other person did not feel comfortable approaching you when he first noticed the problem. Perhaps you seemed critical. In any case, make this an opportunity for both of you to develop closer cooperation in the future by stressing openness.

Once you both agree that something is wrong, allow the other person to share his perception of the problem. Interrupt as little as possible. Use short questions to direct him, such as, "How did that happen? What was your reasoning? "What did you think was happening?

Inviting the other person to critique his own behavior is also effective. Asking how the work could be improved or similar mistakes prevented permits him to make suggestions in a friendly atmosphere. This allows you to see how he examines his performance.

The strong worker is aware of his shortcomings and is working on them even before you point them out. He is pleased to discuss the problem and welcomes your instruction. The weak worker avoids examining the problem and denies his relationship to it.

Your job in offering correction is to help people look at themselves and take responsibility for their own improvement. Provide support and praise them when they improve. Encourage others to ask for your guidance. Get involved when others ask. Listen, pay attention, and show the same sincerity and cooperation you expect from them.

Make your point simply and directly. Make sure that you both are talking about the same subject. Restate your opinion and be done with it. If you find yourself in the same situation over and over again with the same person, then you have to consider if the other person is correctable. You should state this concern directly and see if doing so frees the other person to cooperate with you. If the situation cannot be corrected, you need to decide if it is in your best interest to have that person working for you.

The people who have the most trouble correcting others don't want to spend the time it requires and tend to see employees as things to be managed, not as people. No one rules successfully by fiat. When you give demanding, impersonal orders, other people may agree to your face but do whatever they can get away with when your back is turned.

Fear is a poor motivator. It inspires caution without introspection and makes people seek choices that limit their exposure rather than encouraging them to contribute their best. Growing requires risk, and fear inhibits this.

If you want others to work without constant supervision, give them the freedom to make mistakes without the threat of retaliation. Shouting and fright tactics won't make a sullen worker conform or free a reluctant person to give his best. People generally adapt to threats by becoming inefficient, not more productive.

When you're done, thank the other person for listening. Reassure him of your continued support and belief in his worth. If you have just put the other person on trial and are now giving him a last chance, it is especially important to do this. Expressing your positive belief at a time like this can make the difference between his sincerely trying or giving up. If you are not willing to give him a second chance to redeem himself, you might as well call it a day right then.

Make future contact easier by scheduling regular follow-up meetings so that you can monitor progress without creating a disturbance. Giving criticism without providing follow-up is poor management and reflects the manager's inability to see a project to completion. It may also indicate why the work ran into difficulty in the first place.

If your advice has not been accepted or doesn't seem to make any difference, you should deal with your failure to communicate matter-of-factly. Question whether your criticism was wrong or your advice ineffective. Be open about this and bring it up as a way to continue investigating the problem at hand.

If the other person resists accepting responsibility, denies that a problem exists, or refuses to do what needs to be done, his days with you are limited. Don't threaten, don't cajole. This is a time for being resolute, for being surgical in your intention.

There is a limit to the number of chances anyone gets in life, and everyone needs to learn their lessons. Be prepared to be clear in teaching yours by avoiding personal involvement or confusing emotions.

*This article was reprinted with permission from* **Taking Care of Business** *by David Viscott, MD* *(New York: William Morrow & Company, Inc., 1985).*

*David Viscott, MD, is the author of five best-selling books, including* **How to Live with Another Person** *and* **Risking**. *He hosts a popular national radio talk show.*

# Helping Employees Cope with Change

### by Lorraine Schrag, Elyssa Nelson, and Tedi Siminowsky

• In response to community demand, the ABC Child Care Center opened a room for infants. The new program was an instant success and soon had a waiting list. However, staff in the preschool room were less than excited. The director spent so much time in setting up the new room that she barely had time to help the rest of the staff with their problems. In addition, budgets for classroom supplies were cut to the bone in order to equip the new room.

• The head teacher in the four year old room quit after ten years of teaching at Happy Days Nursery School and was replaced by a new teacher. The rest of the teachers were upset that they were not considered for promotion and were threatened by the new teacher who arrived with lots of enthusiasm and new ideas.

• The arrive of the microcomputers was greeted with delight by the children and with despair by the teachers at the Elm Street After School Program. The teachers were intimidated by the computers and were afraid that their rapport with the children would disappear in a rush of arcade fever.

These are three typical examples of change and its impact on staff in child care centers. We teach children in our centers to be flexible, open, and creative. But when change occurs at the center, we often find that it is the adults who are the most inflexible and the most resistant to change. This resistance may manifest itself in anger, anxiety, bitterness, or despair.

Staff members who are unable to adapt to changes in their work environment may react by complaining to their co-workers, thus chipping away at staff morale. They may vent their frustration by refusing to go along with the change. Their anxiety or anger may cause them to perform below their ability. Or they may just quit, or perform so poorly that they end up being fired.

As a director you would like to avoid these reactions to change, but you know that you cannot avoid making changes. Whether your program is an expanding multi-site system or a small, stable nursery school, you will inevitably be introducing some magnitude of change into your organization. So the question is *how can you introduce change without upsetting your staff?*

The following are five suggestions on helping staff cope with change. They deal with ways to select and develop change-oriented staff members, and they offer some nonthreatening ways to introduce change. But implicit in all of them is the message from director to staff, "I value you so much that I'm going to do whatever I can to bring you along with this change."

## #1. Building a Resilient Staff

The most direct way to minimize staff resistance to change is to build a staff that looks upon change as a challenge rather than as a threat. This involves not only including openness to change as a criteria in the selection process but also using staff development opportunities to strengthen the commitment of staff members.

Openness to change is not, of course, a trait that can be readily measured during the selection process. But there are some fairly reliable indicators to watch for. For example, it may be helpful to get candidates talking about what they did and didn't like about their previous jobs. If dealing with changes comes up in the negative category, this may be a meaningful clue as to what to expect. Also, candidates who are free flowing in their thinking, and who have many ideas to talk about other than that they really love kids, are likely to be able to deal well with change.

Exposing candidates to even a small deviation from the norm in the selection process can also demonstrate how they deal with change. For example, having candidates participate in a group interview as opposed to the expected one-on-one interview can show how they handle the stress of the unexpected.

It is important, once a teacher is hired, to carefully observe her during her probationary period to see how she handles change in practice. Observe how well she deals with small changes, such as being asked to change rooms to fill in for absent teachers. Another factor to observe is how comfortable new teachers are in discussing the problems and successes they are experiencing. Openness in discussing such issues is a positive indication that a person is open to change.

On an ongoing basis, any staff development efforts that get staff members more committed to the goals of the organization are likely to yield positive benefits in times of change. The more that staff members believe they are an integral part of the team, the more willing they will be to put up with any discomforts brought on by changes. Staff, on the other hand, who have little commitment to the organization, who are just along for the ride, will react strongly to any inconvenience or stress.

## #2. Avoiding Leadership Blind Spots

When the director of the Elm Street After School Program decided to buy computers for her program, she was sure the idea would succeed. She had researched the educational implications of computers; she had read hundreds of software reviews to be sure she selected programs that were truly educational as well as entertaining; and she tried these programs out on the computers she planned to buy to make sure everything worked as described. She even prepared carefully for breaking the news to the staff by pulling together the statistics and research to bolster her case.

When the teachers greeted her presentation with misgivings, she set up a computer and, with great enthusiasm, showed them "Speller Kong" and "Math Invaders" in action. Two weeks later, with the computers gathering dust on the shelves, the director wondered what had gone wrong—why had the staff opposed her great idea?

What went wrong was that the director had blind spots which prevented her from seeing what was happening. She was so preoccupied with launching *her baby* that she became oblivious to what was bothering the teachers. When teachers showed signs of resistance, the director responded by rolling out more artillery to win them over to her side. Instead, she should have tried to understand their concerns, to see what was happening from their point of view.

More often than not, when teachers resist a new idea they are not so much opposed to the idea itself as they are anxious about the social consequences of the change. They may be concerned with how this change will affect their relationship with the children, whether it will keep them from working closely with teachers they enjoy, whether it will force them outside their comfort zone to work in an area where they lack expertise.

If the director is so preoccupied with the logistics of implementing the change that she fails to see such social and emotional impacts of change, no amount of haranguing on the merits of the idea will overcome teachers' resistance. When signs of resistance appear, the director may find it helpful to talk to concerned staff members on a one-to-one basis to explore their feelings about the change. An alternative is to pull aside teachers who have already bought into the change and ask for their views on what it is that is causing some staff members to fight the idea. Only when the director has overcome her blind spots and seen the root causes of resistance can she begin to work toward successful implementation of the change.

## #3. Keeping Staff Informed

A large measure of the anxiety aroused during a period of change is caused by fear of the unknown. If a director decides to add an infant component and only announces this in a cursory way, staff members may well be consumed with a host of uncertainties: Will teachers be taken from our classrooms to staff the new program? Will this new program receive top priority for any new money for equipment? Will salary increases be put on hold while the new program is getting started?

Most of this anxiety can be dissolved by keeping staff informed both before and after the change. There may well be a temptation to withhold disclosing a plan until it is finalized, with the reasoning that there is no need to get staff all worked up ahead of time. However, more often than not, inklings of this plan will have leaked through the grapevine anyway. Rather than letting these rumors build erroneous fears, it is usually best to keep staff up to speed from the start on developments that will affect them.

When informing staff about an impending change, it is best to fill them in on the big picture. Let them know what has prompted you to think about making the change; how this change fits in with your center's current goals, or how and why you are shifting your goals; and what the advantages and disadvantages are to making the change.

Then, viewing the change from their perspective, describe how you anticipate this change will impact the day-to-day operations of the center and how it will impact them personally. Try to be as candid as possible in addressing any concerns people might have. If there may be some negative or unpredictable consequences, don't try to gloss over or conceal these. When staff find out later that you were less than honest with them, your credibility will be damaged, if not destroyed.

Sometimes it would appear that a new idea or a change in plans or policies is too complex to fully explain to all staff members. When economic pressures force a center to increase enrollment in the preschool rooms from 18 to 20, a detailed budgetary discussion of all the factors and alternatives may well be beyond the grasp of staff members who aren't versed in accounting. So the director may be tempted to say simply, "We need to do this for budgetary reasons—trust me!" If staff members are being forced by this change to work harder for the same pay, they may view this explanation by the director as somewhat less than satisfactory. While the director should not try to razzle dazzle the teachers with fancy charts and figures, she should take the time and trouble to translate the reasons into terms that all staff members can understand.

Helping staff fully understand change is not simply an act of professional courtesy. In general, it is in the best interests of the program to have teachers who understand what they are doing. A person who does not fully comprehend what she is doing will not be a fully productive worker. She will not be able to exercise informed and intelligent judgment on what she is doing. If the After School teachers do not really understand how the computer programs the kids are using work, they will be handicapped in their efforts to help the children learn through computers.

## #4. Involving Staff in the Change Process

An even better way to bring staff along with a change is to have them participate in the process of change. There are two advantages to inviting participation. First, staff who are involved in planning a change have an ego investment in seeing that it succeeds. They will work hard to make *their* plan work. Second, by including staff in the planning process, you are multiplying the size of your solution pool. By having more minds focused on solving a problem, particularly minds of people whose work is

## Who Can Cope with Change?

Some people have the ability to adapt to change, others do not. Larry Wilson, head of the Wilson Learning Corporation, has identified five attitudes shared by those who are best able to deal with change. If your center is likely to experience considerable change, you may want to keep these attitudes in mind as you select and develop your staff:

• **Challenge**—an openness to change. People possessed with this mindset view change as an opportunity, rather than as a threat.

• **Commitment**—a high degree of involvement in what one is doing. A staff member who believes in what the organization is doing, who is committed to the goals of the organization, is likely to be supportive of changes that improve the performance of the organization.

• **Control**—a sense of personal impact on external change. If staff members, through their ongoing relationship with the organization, feel as if they are not powerless in the face of change, that they will be able to influence the course of change, they will be more accepting of change when it occurs.

• **Confidence**—the recognition that no situation puts your personal worth on the line. Confident people are comfortable with who they are, with their faults as well as their strengths, and with others. They tend not to read into activities (such as organizational changes) implications about their worth. They are less inclined to avoid things that they may not do well, and they are more willing to take risks.

• **Connection**—the extent of interpenetration you are willing to establish between yourself, others, and your environment. Interaction with the external environment, or *making connections*, somehow appears to allow a parallel process to take place internally, enabling a person to develop an increasingly sophisticated system of adaptability to change.

---

central to the purpose of the organization, the chances of arriving at a successful conclusion are increased dramatically.

However, for participation to be effective, it must be true participation and not just a gimmick. Including teachers from the preschool room on a committee to plan the new infant room does not constitute participation if the director has already drafted the plans and just wants a rubber stamp approval. Asking for teachers' opinions on the new staffing structure in a staff meeting is not true participation if the director doesn't intend to take seriously what they have to say. Participation only works if those asked to participate *feel* like they *are* participating and not simply playing a game.

There are myriad ways to get people involved in the change process. One common way is to appoint staff members to serve on a task force. If a new head teacher is being selected, having other teachers participate on the screening committee can be very helpful. Having the support and agreement of the teachers who will be working with the new teacher minimizes feelings of resentment and promotes teamwork.

In other instances, however, appointing a committee is a poor excuse for participation. Unless they are given a very specific, achievable charge, committees often become cumbersome and indecisive. When confronted with a thorny problem, a director may achieve the best results by picking staff members' brains on a one-to-one basis or by conducting brainstorming sessions at regular staff meetings.

Other informal types of participation can have valuable results. If a new head teacher is coming in, you can team her up with one or two of the more experienced teachers and ask them to teach her the ropes.

If you are moving to a new space, you can take *field trips* to the new space ahead of time so that teachers can start planning how to use it.

If you are adding an infant component, you can assign different staff members to be in charge of selecting equipment, buying books and materials, and designing the space.

## #5. Providing Support

During a period of change, when staff members typically are most anxious or angry, the director is often the most distracted and, therefore, least available to relieve this tension. An integral part of the process of planning for change should be thinking through how extra support will be provided to staff during this period.

The most basic form of support that can be provided is to publicly acknowledge at the outset that staff members are likely to feel anxious, ignored, angry, or disoriented. Let them know that such feelings do not reflect a weakness on their part, but that they are an inevitable result of a turbulent, uncertain period. Assure them that someone will be available to listen to their concerns, to answer their questions, and to help them in any way they need to survive this traumatic period.

To underline your support, you should strive to maintain, even to increase if necessary, the frequency of staff meetings. You should schedule specific times when staff members know that they can talk to you on a one-to-one basis. If you disappear from the face of the earth, and if standard communication forums are cut off during this period, staff will have limited productive means of expressing their feelings.

You may also need staff members to take on increased responsibilities as you may be distracted and unable to be as involved in the day-to-day operation of the program. If you see this happening, you should not let it occur by default.

To avoid feelings of resentment, let staff members know ahead of time that they are being entrusted with increased responsibilities. Let them know that you are available if they have serious concerns, but that basically you expect them to act independently, and that you trust they can succeed. Then let them go. Don't be a Monday morning quarterback, second guessing all of their decisions. This is not the time to be hypercritical.

You will inevitably find that, having lain all the above groundwork, there will still be some individuals who will need even more direct support. Most individuals do want to deal successfully with change—it's all a part of growing up. As much as they may overtly resist change, there is a spot in them that wants to grow. What you need to do is to go for that spot, to find a way to get them excited about some aspect of what is going on. Encourage them to take that risk, and let them know that you are supporting them all the way.

If you can't get a teacher to work with the computers in the classroom, maybe you could get her to take a computer home to mess around with over the weekend. If you can't convince the cook that the new vegetarian menu is a good idea, maybe you could get her to cooperate if you were able to work a kitchen aide into the budget.

Unfortunately, you will not be able to find that spot with all people. There will be some people who will not be able to deal with change no matter how much preparation and support you provide. They may not give you much feedback about how they are feeling or why they are having a hard time. They won't provide you with anything to hook onto to turn them around. Or they may be passive resisters—they may agree with everything you say but then go out and perform as they always have, totally disregarding the changed expectations.

Before investing too much time, you need to decide whether it would be in the best interests of the program to keep trying to turn these individuals around or to let them go. Sometimes those who are having a hard time with change will recognize that the stress is too much for them, and they will select themselves out of child care. Others will lack such self-insight and will need to be told that both in the interest of the program and of their career they are being asked to leave.

Throughout the process of change, your attitude as the leader in the organization is critical. If you approach change with enthusiasm and confidence, this spirit can infect your staff. If you maintain your focus on the goals of the organization throughout a period of change, people will not lose sight of the ultimate purpose of change.

If you view your role during change as being a facilitator—one who carefully prepares the way, who keeps channels of communication open, who provides support wherever it is needed—you will make the change easier for everyone. If you respect your employees, you will take the time and effort to bring them along.

*Lorraine Schrag is director of the Centinela Hospital Child Care Center in Inglewood, California; Elyssa Nelson is co-director (with her husband, Eric) of the Child Education Center in La Canada, California; and Tedi Siminowsky is child development services coordinator for the US Army Child Development Services in Berlin, West Germany.*

# How to Stimulate Creativity in Your Staff

### by Roger Neugebauer

*"In every mind there are widening regions of creativity if once the spark has been allowed to generate the fire."* —Gardner Murphy

Creativity is a vital ingredient of any successful child care organization. Creativity is needed in the classroom in planning a responsive curriculum, in designing a stimulating environment, and in providing exciting interactions with the children. The management of a center requires creativity in stretching scant resources, in devising fundraising strategies, and in training and motivating staff. A center must be able to respond creatively to changing populations, changing needs, and changing opportunities.

But can a director truly summon forth a flow of creative ideas from the staff? Aren't there a limited number of creative people in the world and, if your staff doesn't have one, you're out of luck? Management consultant Peter F. Drucker answers that creativity is not in short supply:

"Creativity is not the real problem. There are usually more ideas in any organization than can possibly be put to use. . . . What is lacking is management's willingness to welcome ideas, in fact, solicit them."

Starting with the assumption that creativity is a valuable untapped staff resource, **Exchange** surveyed current management literature for ideas on how to unleash this resource. The following guidelines on how to promote creativity were extracted from those works listed at the end of this article.

### Guideline #1. Clearly communicate the task to the group.

It serves no purpose to get the creative juices of staff members flowing if they are all working on solutions to the wrong problem. At the outset, therefore, it is vital to discuss the problem to be addressed with staff members so that everyone shares a common view of what the group's task is. If the problem is slumping enrollments, for example, everyone should understand that the task is to come up with ideas for recruiting more children. Implicit in this common view is not only a consensus on the specific problem at hand but also a shared understanding of the overall goals and philosophies of the center.

### Guideline #2. Provide group members with rich and varied experiences to draw upon.

Creativity seldom involves the creation of a totally new idea. In their classic treatise on organizational theory, **Organizations**, James March and Herman Simon acknowledged that "most innovations in an organization are a result of borrowing rather than invention." Put another way, creativity involves combining conventional ideas in unconventional ways.

Staff members are more likely to come up with creative combinations of ideas if they have a large store of ideas to draw upon in the first place. According to Gardner Murphy, the first two stages in the creative process are the *immersion in some specific medium that gives delight and fulfillment* and the *acquisition of experiences which are then consolidated into an ordered pattern*. The director, therefore, needs to provide staff members with opportunities to immerse themselves in the issue at hand and to acquire firsthand experiences with it.

There are many ways in which this can happen. For example, let's say the task at hand is to develop a nonsexist curriculum for the center. The director could pull together all available literature on nonsexist childrearing and education for staff members to read. Staff members could be encouraged to attend workshops and take courses on the subject. They could experiment with nonsexist curriculum ideas in their classrooms. They could visit other centers known for their nonsexist curriculums. And the director could bring in an outside expert to brainstorm with the staff on the subject.

### Guideline #3. Provide staff members with whatever support and encouragement they need.

There is much that a director can do to provide support for the creative efforts of staff members. He can demonstrate confidence in the abilities of staff members by delegating significant responsibility to them to come up with a solution or innovation. A lack of confidence is communicated when the director retains tight control over the entire process.

Support can be provided by protecting the creative process from interference. If some staff members are meeting during nap time to brainstorm about a problem in the center, the director should see to it that they can proceed without interruption. If teachers need to visit other centers or to attend workshops, the director should bring in substitutes when necessary to free them to go out.

Wherever possible, the director should provide budgetary support for the creative process. He should not be a scrooge when it comes to acquiring resource materials needed to explore an issue in depth. He should recognize that new innovations—such as a family day care network for infants or a drop-in program—will not be given a fair trial if they are restricted by too tight a budget at the outset.

Drucker argues that pennywise budgeting can cripple innovative efforts:

"Budgets for ongoing businesses and budgets for innovative efforts must not only be kept separate, they should be treated differently. Instead of asking 'What is the minimum level of support needed?,' ask 'What is the maximum of good people and key resources which can productively be put to work at this stage?'"

Finally, support can be provided in the form of rewards. When staff members are successful in coming up with a creative solution to a problem, their efforts should be rewarded. This reward could take the form of a special commendation in a staff meeting, a special notice to the board of directors or corporate officers, a monetary bonus, or a private word of appreciation.

### Guideline #4. Be realistic in your expectations.

Drucker cautions that "the assumption must be that the majority of innovative efforts will not succeed." If the director or staff members are operating under the unrealistic expectation that every idea they come up with will be an instant winner, they will soon be surprised and discouraged. If those participating in the process recognize at the outset that maybe nine out of every ten ideas they come up with will not reach fruition, they will be more patient in waiting for those rare successes.

## Guideline #5. Foster a permissive atmosphere for crazy ideas.

One rule in brainstorming sessions is that participants are not allowed to make negative comments about ideas proposed by other participants. The reason for this is that if participants have their ideas shot down in the group, they will become more defensive and stop offering ideas at all or offer only cautious noncontroversial ideas which they know won't be attacked. With negative judgments being withheld, participants are more likely to offer a wide range of ideas.

A director interested in tapping the creative resources of staff members needs to develop among center staff the same openness to ideas which exists in a brainstorming session. Staff members need to feel that their suggestions and ideas are welcomed and valued. They should not be reluctant to share their thoughts out of fear they will be ridiculed, criticized, or ignored.

The director should provide staff members with multiple channels for offering their ideas. Ideas could be sought in staff meetings with a brainstorming format. For those intimidated in group discussions, the director may want to solicit their views in private conversations. Others may not want to share their opinions in public at all but may need the impersonal avenue of a suggestion box.

## Guideline #6. Expose ideas to critical examination.

The vacation from criticism should not last forever. Once staff members are secure enough to risk unlimited speculation, there needs to be a point where ideas proposed are evaluated with a critical eye. "The creative process," explains William J. J. Gordon, "stems from the total personalities, and an attempt to deny the critical element can have no lasting productive effect."

However, there are constructive and nonconstructive ways to offer criticism. For example, if in a staff meeting all suggestions for redesigning the outdoor play area are being reviewed, the tendency of group members may be to select the best suggestion and to reject all the others. In this process, the useful elements or germs of ideas in the nonwinners are often missed.

To avoid this *all-or-nothing* criticism, a number of techniques can be employed. One is to require group members to point out the good aspects of a proposal as well as the negative ones when offering criticism. A related approach is to expect critics to offer suggestions on how they would modify a rejected proposal. Finally, an opponent of an idea could be expected to offer an alternative to the idea he is opposing.

## Guideline #7. Allow staff members to concentrate on problems that especially interest them.

According to Harry Levinson, an organization is best served when it "permits people to seize and develop those challenges and problems which most excite their curiosity." A director, for example, could hold a staff meeting at which all staff members brainstorm about the center's major problems to be solved and opportunities to be seized. From this discussion a priority list of tasks to be addressed could be compiled, and each staff member could be allowed to choose one or two tasks to focus attention on.

One consequence of this approach, Levinson notes, is that staff members may be interested in an issue that "may not at the moment be of major concern to the organization." This drawback is compensated for by the fact that "the freedom to follow one's interest stimulates a flow of ideas." This flow of ideas on a range of issues would be far more useful to the center in the long run than the trickle of ideas that might result if all staff members were required to be creative about a crucial problem that did not interest most of them.

## Guideline #8. Allow staff members to proceed at their own pace and in their own way.

Individuals cannot turn their creative process on and off like a faucet. Everyone has their own pattern or pace for evoking creativity. One person gets a mental block about problems while on the job but finds that ideas come to him in a flood when he is jogging. Another has no success until late at night when he relaxes in his favorite chair with a cup of tea. Most people need to take a mental vacation somewhere in the process—they need to follow a period of intense immersion in a problem with a totally new activity where the conscious mind focuses on something different.

As often as not, the solution that did not come when a person was deliberately trying to think of it will pop into his mind when he is thinking about something else. This unpredictable, highly individualized nature of the creative process must be taken into account by a director seeking to make it happen.

**Guideline #9. Don't foil brainstorming sessions with preliminary termination.**

Guideline #8 applies to the creative process as it occurs in individuals, and Guideline #9 applies to the creative process as it occurs in groups. The rules for these two settings differ considerably. In a group setting, it becomes more important to force the process along somewhat.

After an hour or so of intense concentration in a brainstorming session, many staff members will be showing signs of fatigue and may look for an end to the session or at least a prolonged coffee break. Gordon argues, however, that generally such a break should be avoided. He contends that it takes a long time for the creative process to get rolling. To take a break in midstream "would interrupt the continuity of thought . . . and would allow the subconscious imaginative energy to congeal." To reach a satisfactory conclusion, Gordon finds, brainstorming sessions must often continue for three hours.

One means of combatting fatigue without terminating the meeting is comedy. When the energy level is drooping, a group member can make a satirical or offbeat suggestion to allow the discussion to digress from the intense level for a few minutes. According to Gordon, "after a few minutes of laughter group members are usually ready again for rigorous and energetic performance."

Gordon also sees some advantage to fatigue setting in. It can force participants to let their guard down and to abandon themselves to taking longer chances. Group members may start *swinging for the fences*. Such a swing can be the culmination of protracted imaginative effort—not merely a wild blow, but a highly concentrated mental act tending to reveal a creative solution.

**Guideline #10. Don't underestimate the value of success.**

Nothing will help the flow of creativity along better than some early and continuing successes. If a director sets out to foster a creative spirit, staff members may initially react with disinterest or pessimism. If the group experiences an early success—if it comes up with a creative solution to a problem—this early uncertainty may be replaced by interest and excitement. If success is long in coming, the uncertainty may deteriorate into frustration and cynicism.

With this in mind, directors might want to focus on problems of minor magnitude early on to improve the likelihood of success. Gordon also suggests that, until the initial success is realized, no meeting should end on a note of defeat. The director may want to hold off on some promising suggestions until the end of a session if it is not going well. Or he may want to summarize at the end all the promising leads which were brought up during the session.

Having tasted early success, staff members usually will be more patient in waiting for additional victories. But these victories must occur from time to time if participants are going to maintain faith in the effort. One frequent shortcoming is that lots of creative ideas are proposed, but none of them are ever implemented. Murphy identifies *hammering out* as the final stage in the creative process. When the group comes up with a creative solution to a problem, its work is not done. The solution must be worked out in detail, adopted to the center's exact needs, and implemented. The creative process does not end in success when the solution is created, but only when the problem is in fact solved.

## References

Drucker, Peter F. **Management: Tasks, Responsibilities, Practices.** New York: Harper and Row, 1974.

Drucker, Peter F. "The Big Power of Little Ideas," **Harvard Business Review**, May-June 1964.

Gordon, William J. J. "Operational Approach to Creativity," **Harvard Business Review**, November-December 1956.

Levinson, Harry. **The Exceptional Executive.** Cambridge: Harvard University Press, 1968.

March, James, and Herman Simon. **Organizations.** New York: John Wiley and Sons, 1958.

Murphy, Gardner. **Human Potentialities.** New York: Basic Books, 1958.

# The Ten Best Ways to Reward Good Work

### advice from Michael LeBoeuf

I was browsing in our local bookstore the other day when one title caught my eye: **GMP: The Greatest Management Principle in the World**. Not since **The Ten Minute Manager** has one book promised so much and cost so little. For only $6.95 you could learn how to "simplify problems, stimulate productivity, boost loyalty, increase effective behavior, improve quality . . . and much more."

Being the ultimate sucker that I am, I plunked down some of my scant resources and headed home to discover the Holy Grail, the Northwest Passage, the cure for the common cold, the answer to all supersvisory headaches. Of course, the minute I left the bookstore I realized that I'd probably thrown my money away on another book like **The Ten Minute Manager**, with its inflated promises and deflated answers.

I was surprised and happy to discover that **GMP** did have redeeming social value. While the book is not quite the cure-all it promises to be, its author, Michael LeBoeuf, does provide valuable, no-nonsense advice on motivating employees.

To end the suspense (and to save you $6.95), LeBoeuf claims the greatest management principle in the world is (drum roll): *the things that get rewarded get done.* LeBoeuf suggests, therefore, that the key to improving organizations is to provide the proper link between performance and rewards. A manager's goal should be to find ways to reward the types of performance that improve the organization's productivity and quality. Along the way LeBoeuf identified, in order of importance, the following ways to reward proper performance.

## Reward #1: Money

Right off the bat LeBoeuf hits us below the belt, right? Child care center budgets can barely support anything above a minimal salary structure, and here he's telling us that money is the #1 reward. We might as well skip ahead to numbers 2 through 9.

Not true. While LeBoeuf would undoubtedly agree that our wage structure is a handicap when it comes to achieving optimum performance, there is no need to throw in the towel. According to LeBoeuf, the key is to provide a meaningful link between pay and performance. In other words, if teachers who perform better are paid better, there will be a positive incentive for teachers to improve their performance.

Indeed, the economics of child care do not give us much room to maneuver when it comes to rewarding performance monetarily. But it may be worthwhile to analyze how you allocate your resources. Is there a link in your salary structure between pay and performance? Are your best teachers the highest paid? When you free up additional money for salaries, do divide it up equally, or do you direct most of the new money to your best performers? In short, is there any financial reason for a teacher in your center to strive to improve her performance?

After going through an analysis such as this, some directors have concluded that organizational performance would be improved if the center's salary structure was readjusted to reward the best teachers. In these centers, top teachers earn considerably more than the average and below average performers. While not a perfect solution, this practice has resulted in a higher level of motivation and retention among the centers' best performers.

Another practice that is becoming increasingly popular in child care centers is performance bonuses. Centers set aside a modest amount of money for bonuses, and then award it, on anywhere from a monthly to an annual basis, to staff members identified as top performers. While the bonuses awarded are not exactly earth-shaking ($25 to $100 is typical), centers that have experimented with this approach are convinced that they have stimulated an improvement in performance. (Note: In the September 1986 issue of **Exchange**, a variety of bonus plans used by centers will be described in detail).

## Reward #2: Recognition

Author Laurence Peter once observed, "There are two kinds of egotists: Those who admit it and the rest of us." For this reason, LeBoeuf proposes that recognition can be a powerful incentive—in some cases an even more powerful incentive than money. It is amazing, he notes, how hard people will work when the payoff is feeling appreciated and important.

How do you reward with recognition? According to LeBoeuf you need to be creative in coming up with ideas that will appeal to the people who work for you. But to get you started, he lists some popular examples:

- Employee-of-the-month awards
- Certificates of achievement
- Newsletter stories
- Changes in job title
- Public praise
- Congratulatory letter
- Awards at a banquet
- Status symbols such as tiepins, rings, or a better parking place

## Reward #3: Time Off

Paid time off can be an incentive—if it is tied to performance. Just as some centers award monetary bonuses for top performance, you can award time off for predetermined measures of accomplishment.

For example, you could award a Friday afternoon off to the staff member in each room who exhibits the most appropriate interaction behavior with children in a round of observations. Or you could award a day off to the teacher who scores most highly in evaluations turned in by parents.

## Reward #4: Ownership

This reward is based on the hypothesis that *employees who become owners behave like owners*. In other words, those who own a part of the company have a stake in its success, and, therefore, are more likely to behave in ways that improve productivity and profits.

This hypothesis seems to have some basis in fact. A University of Michigan study found that firms with some worker ownership averaged profits one and a half times greater than those of conventional companies in their field.

In the child care world, awarding a piece of the action is not so easy. Non profit centers cannot by law distribute ownership to private individuals. In addition, most for profit centers in this country are privately held, i.e. they do not have shares of stock to distribute to employees.

That is not to say that centers cannot come up with some systems that offer the motivational equivalent of ownership. For example, having salary levels tied to center profitability may enhance staff members' concern for the performance of the center. In a non profit center, salaries could possibly be adjusted based upon the achievement of pre-established budgetary targets. In a similar vein, year end bonuses could be distributed to employees if profits exceed a set level.

Other practices may increase the sense of involvement of teachers. Such practices might include involving teachers in the selection of members of their team, seeking teachers' input on decisions about fees and enrollments, and including teachers on a board of directors. Such practices may indeed be motivational. However, since they do not provide a direct link between organizational performance and personal rewards (helping to select the best teacher to work with may make your work easier and more fulfilling, but it won't directly effect your paycheck), their impact is less direct.

## Reward #5: Favorite Work

Give people more of the tasks they enjoy doing (spending one to one time with children) as a reward for good performance. At the same time, excuse them from assignments they dislike (end of the day cleanup). Since people usually enjoy doing the things they do best, this is a great way to improve the performance of your best performers.

## Reward #6: Advancement

With the current staffing shortage, you can't afford to lose good people who leave because there is no chance for them to advance. Giving staff opportunities to grow within the organization can be a critical reward to be able to offer.

Typically, advancement within the organization means a full-fledged promotion to a position with supervisory or managerial responsibility. If, as is often the case, your center does not have such positions available, you need to be creative in providing growth opportunities. For example, if you have a teacher aide who has been improving steadily, but no lead teacher position is available, you could reward her with a special assignment (such as organizing a parent evaluation) for which she is paid a set amount of additional money.

## Reward #7: Freedom

Freedom and autonomy on the job can be very effective rewards. In essence you tell people, "Do the job right and you can be your own boss." This can be motivating for employees who take their career seriously. As LeBoeuf quotes one worker, "I don't mind being pushed, as long as I can steer."

You can reward teachers who have been performing well by giving them increased control over how their classroom is run. They can be given a budget for supplies and equipment and told to use their own judgement as to how to spend it. You can give creative teachers freedom to develop a plan for a new idea they propose (for redesigning the toddler room, for implementing a new curriculum, for adding a school age program).

## Reward #8: Personal Growth

For teachers who care about what they are doing, personal growth is a crucial reward. The way to keep them loyal and performing well is to make their work interesting and to give them the opportunity to learn new skills and grow in their chosen field.

Personal growth rewards can be given in two basic ways. First, give people new tasks that challenge their creative ability and provide them with the chance to prove themselves and grow. Second, reward top performers with training and educational opportunities. For example, paying teachers to attend a state AEYC meeting, or enrolling them in a course that excites them, or helping them set up visits to several other centers in the area could all be used as personal growth incentives.

## Reward #9: Fun

Child care calls for long hours of hard work. It's also very important work—being entrusted with the care of children is an awesome responsibility. It is often work that is fraught with strong emotions—anger, guilt, and sadness to name a few. It is serious work that is usually taken so seriously that there is no room for fun and relaxation.

For teachers to be effective they must be relaxed and happy with what they are doing—if not they will turn an exciting developmental program into a watching-the-clock babysitting service.

Building fun into the workplace as a reward for good work makes a great deal of sense. This does not mean telling jokes at staff meetings or pulling pranks in the teachers lounge. It does mean taking time out for a teacher's birthday party, celebrating a successful month with a party at the corner pizza parlor, or rigging up a sound system so that teachers can play good music at different times of the day.

## Reward #10: Prizes

The way to reward performance with prizes is limited only by imagination. Family dinners paid by the center, sports or theater tickets, and gift certificates are common examples of prize incentives. Prizes can be utilized to reward attendance, longevity, recruitment of children or teachers, or successful completion of one-shot tasks.

So these are Michael LeBoeuf's ten ways of rewarding good work. He suggests numbers 1 and 2 are far and away the most important. You may want to evaluate these in terms of your own setting to see which types of rewards will be the most meaningful for your staff.

*Michael LeBoeuf is a management consultant who, in addition to* **GMC: The Greatest Management Principle in the World** *(New York: Berkley Books, 1985), has written* **Working Smart: How to Accomplish More in Half the Time** *(New York: Warner Books, 1979).*

# A Reappraisal of Praise

### ideas of Richard E. Farson

*Writing in the September-October 1963 issue of **Harvard Business Review**, Richard E. Farson questions the effectiveness of praise as a motivational technique. His observations about the effects of praise are as follow:*

**The Effect of Praise**

• *Praise is not only of limited and questionable value as a motivator, but it may in fact be experienced as threatening.*

People usually react to praise with discomfort, uneasiness, and defensiveness. Typical responses tend to play down or deny the praise: "Well, **we** like it" or "It was just luck" or "Well, I do the best I can." For a number of reasons praise is often perceived as a threat. To begin with, praise is, in fact a form of evaluation, any any evaluation is likely to make a person uncomfortable and defensive. When you evaluate a person you are trying to motivate him, to move him in a certain direction, to change him. This implies a negative judgment about the way the person is now, about his identity. So even though praise may only imply that one should change a bit in the direction one is already going, it does imply change, and it therefore may be as threatening as a negative evaluation.

Praise is also viewed as a threat because of our tendency to sugarcoat blame with praise. Supervisors are often instructed to sandwich in bits of negative feedback with huge doses of praise. "Your lesson plan really went well today, but try not to talk down to the children. Keep up the good work!" We have become so conditioned by the use of praise as psychological candy, that when we are praised, we automatically get ready for the shock, the reproof.

• *Rather than functioning as a bridge between people, praise may actually serve to establish distance between them.*

We talk a good deal about wanting to be close to people, but when you come right down to it, there really are very few people whom we want to be close to. It is necessary to be able to maintain distance from people, to keep a little free space around ourselves—psychological elbow room—especially in a society which fills our lives with so many contacts. In the search for techniques to establish distance between ourselves and others, we find that praise is one of the most effective, simply because, when we evaluate people we are not likely to gain emotional proximity to them. Compare the effects of praise with other behaviors—for instance listening to another or revealing your feelings to another—to see if praise doesn't tend to hold off, to separate, while the other behaviors tend to include, to embrace.

• *Instead of reassuring a person as to his worth, praise may be an unconscious means of establishing the superiority of the praiser.*

Praise can be a means of gaining status over another by establishing the fact that one is capable of sitting in judgment. Status is important to all of us, and though the person being evaluated may feel that the praise is threatening, or diminishing, the praiser himself has increased his psychological size, or if he praises an inferior, has claimed or reinforced his status.

## Alternatives to Praise

It is when we want to develop initiative, creativity, judgment, and problem-solving ability in people that praise fails us most. To liberate these qualities in people we need to rely on internal motivation. We need to make people feel that they are free of our control. We may need to establish a more egalitarian atmosphere, and sometimes we need to create closeness with superiors. But if praise produces status differences, not equality; if it creates distance, not closeness; if it is felt as a threat not as a reassurance; then how do you establish a free, accepting yet close relationship that will encourage independent judgment, effective decisions, and creative actions? Two approaches may be effective:

• *Being honest—showing some of yourself to another person, transparently exhibiting some of your own feelings and attitudes.*

Being honest is not easy because from early childhood we have learned to play roles which mask our feelings, as if being honest about them would only hurt others and destroy relationships. Actually, it is the other way around; we mask our feelings so that we will not have too many close—and possibly burdensome—relationships. The inevitable consequence of exposing and sharing feelings is emotional closeness. The times when one can risk vulnerability are perhaps life's richest moments—but are not often psychologically comfortable moments.

• *Empathetic listening—to try to see how the world looks to the other person and to communicate this understanding to him.*

This empathetic, non-evaluative listening responds to the person's feelings as well as to his words. It implies no evaluation or judgment. It simply conveys an understanding of what the person is feeling and attempting to communicate; and his feelings and ideas are accepted as being valid for him, if not for the listener.

It is difficult to listen because if we allow ourselves to see the world through another's eyes, we run the risk of changing ourselves, our own point of view. And, as previously indicated, change is something we try to avoid.

But at times when we do want to develop creativity and self-confidence in others, when we do want to establish a close relationship in which the other person feels free "to be himself," then expressing our feelings honestly and listening sensitively may be far more helpful than offering praise.

---

*Richard E. Farson is director of Western Behavioral Sciences Institute in La Jolla, California.*

# How Did You Manage That?
# A Closer Look at Staff Guidance

### by Pauline Davey Zeece

At a time when society demands quick fixes and simple solutions to complex problems, a search for the ideal model of staff management is inviting. A stroll through the business section of your local library or bookstore will afford the opportunity to polish your passion for excellence or mull over megatrends for the next millennium. The truly brave can learn to dance with giants or ponder the leadership secrets of Attila the Hun! While such resources may offer insight into management, none presents *the* answer to effective staff guidance.

In reality, there is no single right answer. Perhaps this is because staff guidance by its nature is a dynamic process. It is action and growth oriented. As such, it is based on the assumption that everyone in an organization is constantly changing and that all can benefit from growth opportunities.

Although there may not be one right answer, Caruso and Fawcett (1986) suggest that the quality of early childhood programming can only be maintained and improved when administrators have a realistic understanding of how workers grow and develop in their roles as caregivers and teachers.

**New Thoughts about Old Ideas**

With little time (and usually less money), where can directors turn for direction in staff guidance? Where can administrators obtain information about staff growth and development?

Surprisingly, the answer may be closer than you think. Staff guidance can be optimized when it functions within the guidelines of developmentally appropriate practice. As with children, the concept of developmental appropriateness has two dimensions: age and stage appropriateness and individual appropriateness (Bredekamp, 1986).

### And How Did You Grow: Age and Caregiving

Each of us brings to our respective jobs the collective experiences of a lifetime. And part of these experiences include the attitudes we have developed toward work roles.

Because attitudes about work roles are often formed during a child's early years, younger and older workers may vary in their initial expectations about a variety of things related to child care work.

For example, some older workers may at first feel uneasy when a three year old calls them by their first name, as such behavior may appear impudent. A young beginning director may experience discomfort when taking disciplinary action with a worker who is the same age as a parent or grandparent.

Developmentally appropriate practice, then, does not dictate change based on the birth cohort of staff. Rather, it requires that directors develop a sensitivity about the relative effects of age and incorporate this awareness into a staff management style.

Allowing and encouraging staff to share their perspectives based on when they were born and how they were treated as children builds rapport and strengthens programming.

### Developmental Stages of Child Care Workers

Understanding stages of child care work can also be a part of age appropriate practice. Nearly 20 years ago, Katz (1972) delineated changes that teachers of young children experience.

She labeled these changes as developmental stages which include:

Stage I — Survival
Stage II — Consolidation
Stage III — Renewal
Stage IV — Maturity

**The survival stage.** Survival is a very real part of child care work. Not only is the job physically demanding, but it is also psychologically intense. Bonda, a beginning infant/toddler teacher recalls:

*"The first months were terrible. I would go home at night and collapse. The first few days I couldn't even find the bathroom. By the second week, several toddlers had attached to me — so even though I knew where it was, I couldn't get away to use it. I remember telling my roommate that I was so tired, even my hair hurt!"*

Additionally, when a teaching or caregiving assignment is changed, an experienced and successful teacher may be thrown back into survival mode. For example, although an infant teacher may know many of the mechanics and policies of a program, she or he may discover that five year olds bring their own special kind of pandemonium to a child care job.

Length of time in the survival mode may be less the second or third time around, but the feelings of panic are oftentimes the same. It may be that beginning directors go through this very difficult survival stage, too!

Survival mode teachers need:

• Assurance that what they are feeling and experiencing is not unusual or wrong.

• Specific, detailed, ongoing information about the mechanics of the job they are expected to do.

• Feedback from colleagues and administrators. They need assurance that they can and will survive.

**The consolidation stage.** "I not only survived, but I am making a difference" could be the slogan of consolidation mode teachers and caregivers. Ronnie, a teacher of four year olds, talks about his second six months at a child care center:

*"At first I thought it was because I was male. I couldn't tell anyone how I felt. How could I say that four year olds were making me crazy? But it got better, especially when I figured out that the world wouldn't end when things didn't get done exactly. . . . I think the turning point for me was when they (other teachers) started asking me about my science table instead of just asking me to help move stuff."*

During the consolidation period, workers feel more organized and secure with everyone — children, parents, and colleagues. The focus of energy turns from managing panic to planning programs.

Working as a team member is more physically and psychologically rewarding. This is the time when teachers begin to build a repertoire of skills. It is also a time when their sense of themselves as competent teachers and caregivers is established.

Consolidation mode teachers need:

• Continued feedback and reassurance from administrators.

• Encouragement or empowerment to solve their own problems — they are best directed to exchange solutions and ideas with others.

• Additional information about individual differences and specific behavior management techniques.

**The renewal stage.** Introspection is the hallmark of the renewal stage. At this time, workers possess the security and self-confidence necessary to realistically examine their professional strengths and weaknesses. Molly, a veteran nursery school teacher, comments:

*"I have come to the point in my life when I want more . . . but I'm not quite sure what more is yet. I know I'm good with children — I hear that from parents all the time. But there are days when I just go through the motions. It may sound egotistic but I'm good enough at this that other people can't tell. . . . But I can tell and that's what bothers me."*

Renewal mode teachers oftentimes need exposure to innovation. If they have not had the opportunity to engage in advocacy efforts, this may also be a time when this is important. More than new equipment, they seek new ideas and new ways to think about old (or enduring) problems.

This is often the stage wherein the teacher-specialist emerges. Teacher preference, talent, and experience mesh to create a unique teacher identity. Stevens and King (1976) suggest that workers in this stage should be encouraged to build on and extend emerging specializations.

Renewal mode teachers need:

• Feedback and recognition from administrators.

• Opportunities which encourage their growth as professionals and specialists.

• Opportunities to function as team leaders and mentors for beginning teachers.

**The maturity stage.** If renewal mode teachers are mentors for new workers, maturity mode teachers are mentors for the profession. Mature teachers and caregivers are committed to quality early life experiences for every child.

Maturity is not necessarily a function of age or even of longevity involvement in the field. This is the time when interest and involvement in advocacy emerges or matures.

The fifth and final stage of professionalism is **the influential stage**. According to Vander Ven (1988), few reach this final plateau which is characterized by many years of experience in multiple roles in child care work.

Workers in the influential stage are often recognized as state and national leaders. They may be directors of well known, model service programs. Influential stage workers are self-directed and feel comfortable with leadership and authority. These are the people who set the pace, first in their own thinking and then in their professional endeavors.

## Individual Differences

Staff guidance techniques can also be enhanced when directors are sensitive to individual differences, most obviously differences in temperament and cognitive style.

*A Closer Look at Temperament*

Even as very young children, people display distinct differences. As people mature, they learn to act in socially appropriate ways. They also show very basic differences in their approach to life and in their individual temperaments. Keirsey and Bates (1978) have proposed temperament categories which may be applied or extended to those who work in child care. Workers in these categories may be conceptualized as adventurous, responsible, intuitive thinking, and intuitive feeling.

**The adventurous worker.** Adventurous workers are spontaneous, fun-loving, and impulsive by nature. They oftentimes are interested in a wide variety of things and may have difficulty when organization or preparation is left solely to them. Completing tasks or unplanned delays may also be difficult for workers with this temperament.

What they do well is help children and colleagues see the world as an ongoing adventure. Boldness, cleverness, and performance are what many adventurous workers pride themselves on: they feel appreciated when these qualities are noted.

**The responsible worker.** Even as very young children, responsible workers thrive on a predictable, scheduled world. They respond most favorably when the surroundings are ordered so that the same thing happens at the same time each day.

Of all the temperament styles, this is the most susceptible to conflict at work. This makes sense considering the disruption that such conflict often brings. Carefulness, thoroughness, and accuracy are valued by this group.

The predictable, dependable nature of responsible temperament workers can be deceptive, for insecurity may be buried beneath an outwardly competent surface. Administrator approval is highly valued, and it is important not to place unrealistic expectations or pressures on people with this temperament style.

**The intuitive thinking worker.** Intuitive thinking workers may seem solemn. They may prefer standing back and watching things happen instead of becoming actively involved in activities.

This should not be mistaken for a lack of interest or lack of intellectual ability. Actually, as a group, intuitive workers are high achievers who enjoy and seek out challenges in a variety of ways.

Conflict may appear if these workers lose respect for administrators who are not logical or fair in their demands or who issue rules that are not warranted by the circumstances. The ideal child care environment for these workers is one in which the right to question is valued and appreciated.

**The intuitive feeling worker.** Intuitive feeling workers are sometimes called empathic. They are usually happy, but they need reassurance that they are valued because they are sensitive people.

There are wide differences in the behavior of workers within this temperament style. For example, introverted and extroverted empathic workers are very different. For the extrovert, life among people is filled with pleasant interaction as these workers seem to have a charm that draws people to them. For the introvert, there may be some difficulty communicating, especially in new circumstances.

Intuitive feeling workers are quite responsive to administrators who are accepting, who allow for expression of feelings, and who genuinely respond to their ideas and opinions.

*What Do You Think about That?*

Another important way in which people differ is called **cognitive style**. Cognitive styles are consistent individual differences in the ways workers organize and process information as they perform their jobs. However, cognitive style does not imply a level of intelligence or even the content of cognition. Rather, it represents the strategies and preferences a worker uses in thinking through problems.

Messick (1976) proposed that all people utilize cognitive styles or conceptual tempos. Accordingly, these tempos are either **reflective** or **impulsive** in nature. The worker who uses a reflective style takes a longer time to solve a problem, but is more accurate.

In a child care setting, reflective workers might respond more positively when given time to think about upcoming changes before they occur. They may be silent during a heated staff meeting, only to come up with a brilliant solution after everyone has left the room. Reflective workers function best in a planned, ordered, and predictable environment.

Impulsive workers respond swiftly to situations. They are quick to answer and to analyze. Although they solve problems more quickly, they may make more errors. This does not necessarily mean that impulsive workers are irresponsible or ineffective. It only implies that they are cognitive risk takers and are able to brainstorm about immediate solutions. They are more likely to spontaneously contribute during a staff meeting. Impulsive workers may be more influenced by authority figures. In general, they have more highly developed social skills and function best in an environment which provides opportunities for discussion and fosters the notion that there are many right or acceptable ways to do things.

## So . . .

Regardless of the ages, stages, or individual differences among workers, it is clear that competent and caring interaction enhances the administrator-worker relationship. Also, like all general descriptions, these categories, stages, and models are meant to be used only as a guide to a better understanding of people. All workers are unique; they will not fit any of these profiles perfectly.

The fact that people do have predictable similarities, as well as challenging differences, has important implications for child care administrators.

First, this makes the best case for utilizing developmentally appropriate practice with adults, as well as children, within a child care setting.

Second, it should be reassuring to directors that behavior once thought to be the result of poor management may actually be traits or development characteristics of workers.

Third, although administrators may not be responsible for workers' age, stage, temperament, or cognitive style, their reactions to such things may have important consequences for staff guidance and professional development.

Staff guidance is an important and integral part of successful program administration. When it is steeped within developmentally appropriate practice, it affords all involved the opportunity to grow, develop, and prosper.

## References

Bredekamp, S. (1986). **Developmentally appropriate practice.** Washington, DC: National Association for the Education of Young Children.

Caruso, J., and Fawcett, M. (1986). **Supervision in early childhood practice: A developmental perspective.** New York: Teachers College Press.

Katz, L. (1972). Developmental stages of preschool teachers. **Elementary School Journal**, 73 (1), 50-54.

Keirsey, D., and Bates, M. (1978). **Please understand me: Character and temperament types.** Del Mar, CA: Prometheus Nemesis Books.

Messick, S. (1976). **Individuality in learning.** San Francisco, CA: Jossey-Bates.

Stevens, J., and King, E. (1976). **Administering early childhood programs.** Boston: Little, Brown and Company.

Vander Ven, K. (1988). Pathways to professional effectiveness for early childhood educators. In B. Spodek, O. Saracho, and D. Peters (editors), **Professionalism and the early childhood practitioner.** New York: Teachers College Press.

*Pauline Davey Zeece is director of the Child Development Laboratory at the University of Nebraska–Lincoln and assistant professor in the Department of Human Development and the Family.*

# Managing Teacher Performance While Walking Around

## by Kay Albrecht

Every director knows that much of her time is spent on the move — checking on the timbre and staffing of classrooms, responding to crying or especially noisy episodes, giving messages to teachers, checking the status of supplies, and attending to numerous other details. It often feels like nothing has been accomplished because there have been so many interruptions and distractions!

On the other hand, directors who spend time in and around their centers, who are visible, who are seen as empathetic to teachers' needs and the demands of the classroom, who help out on occasion when times get tough, and who provide technical assistance in problem solving, are viewed by teachers as both supportive to the teaching role and successful in the director role.

Figuring out how to manage performance while walking around is a good strategy for insuring that the day will not pass by without accomplishing something. Capturing the time spent on the move, making it count, can have positive consequences for program quality and teacher satisfaction.

**Develop a note taking system.**

Gathering and retaining information is the first step in managing it. As directors move around their centers, comments are made by teachers, problems are identified, information about families is mentioned, and observations about teacher competence and performance are noted. Few directors can keep all this information straight and remember what needs to be done with it when they get back to their desks.

A good note taking system is a must— portable, accessible, and ALWAYS at hand. Some systems that might work include a clipboard with blank paper, a steno book, or a message pad.

One enterprising director who heard this suggestion uses a telephone message book. The result is two copies of any note — one to keep and one to pass on to the appropriate person to take action (such as the janitor, the cook, or another teacher), to file for later action (like ordering more paint or contact paper), or to use as part of the competency data collected for teacher conferences.

How will teachers feel about you taking notes as you pass through? At first there may be some sensitivity. Discuss what you are doing and why with teachers before you begin to take notes.

Then, make sure your first few notes are ones that result in action, like making suggestions on how to deal with a child's behavior or fixing broken equipment. Over time, teachers will become accustomed to you collecting information in writing.

One note of caution — this note taking system should not take the place of formal request systems like maintenance requests or vacation requests. It is designed to help the director capture the useful information that is available for the taking as she walks around the center.

## Make the time spent walking around serve a purpose.

As they walk around, directors are gathering information — if not directly, then indirectly. Often, such observations serve to pinpoint "problems" and to identify training or management needs. By focusing the time spent walking around, the type and range of information gathered can be broadened and the usability of information collected increased. When viewed as an opportunity to observe a teacher's competence in a certain skill area, to gather information about classroom dynamics (either between children or among staff), or to identify training interests or needs, walking around becomes a powerful information gathering tool.

At least two strategies for focusing the time spent walking around come to mind. One entails starting the day with an agenda. A long list of action items might be on your list — checking the status of classroom cleanliness, looking for cues about teacher satisfaction (or dissatisfaction), reviewing equipment needs, observing teaching teamwork, evaluating the effectiveness of transitions from indoors to outdoors, observing the play of a child who is having problems, etc. Use your note taking system to prompt your observations by writing down your agenda and checking off the items as information is collected.

A less directed technique borrows from child development observational strategies — take anecdotal notes as you walk around, pausing for two or three minutes here and there to make sure your notes are thorough.

Anecdotal notes have some advantages — they are records of what you see, not of what you think about what you see. The distinction is a useful one because it prevents drawing conclusions based on limited information and saves the analysis of the observation for a later time. Anecdotal notes create opportunities for you to gather information across time, preventing snap judgments and premature conclusions. The disadvantage of anecdotal notes is that they require further work. Analysis of the notes must take place to synthesize, draw conclusions, identify training needs, and so on.

## Do something with your notes.

A major pitfall to accomplishing anything as a director is the overwhelming feeling that everything must be done by one person. The conclusion of every walk should result in action.

If your walk identifies additional work needed by the custodial crew, copy your observations, add the necessary instructions to fix the problem, then route the message to the custodian. If you identified a teacher training need, drop your notes into the teacher's file to include in her next competency evaluation. Taking action promptly reduces the number of things on your plate and allows you to feel a sense of accomplishment.

If you chose to make anecdotal notes, doing something with your notes is a two-step process. The first step is to analyze your notes, drawing conclusions and identifying implications. The second step is doing something with the analysis.

Don't get bogged down in the analysis step. Some anecdotal notes serve only as documentation of impressions, confirmations of perceptions, or examples of experiences and can either be kept together in a file or sorted out into classroom files for future reference.

## Use walking around time as a chance to increase communication.

In busy centers, communication among teachers and between directors and teachers is often a casualty of the time crunch. Seizing moments as you walk around can substantially increase the amount of communication that occurs, particularly if you time your moments well.

A personal example — a preschool teacher recently submitted her resignation. The day after I got the resignation, I spent about 20 minutes with the rest of the preschool teaching team after most of the children were asleep for nap. I asked questions about the characteristics and skills the teachers wanted to see in a replacement. I asked them to think about it overnight and returned the next day for about 10 minutes at nap time to continue the discussion.

On the third day, I went back again and asked the teachers to commit their thoughts to paper — 15 minutes later, I left the classroom with a list of the personal and competency requirements for the vacant position from the teachers' perspective.

Another note of caution — if you plan to use walking around time for increasing communication, it must be well timed. Interrupting a busy teacher in the classroom to increase communication will not be well received. Instead, enter as an unobtrusive observer and wait for a free moment. Or, become familiar enough with each classroom's daily schedule to identify when teachers are likely to have a few minutes of time to talk to you.

Managing while walking around is a technique for keeping in touch — with children, staff, and your facility — and for connecting yourself to the day-to-day happenings of the center. It is also a technique for gathering and managing the tremendous amount of information available through observation. Further, it can increase the amount and quality of communication between you and your teachers.

*Kay Albrecht, Ph.D., a senior partner in Child Care Management Associates, Houston and Dallas, specializes in consulting on marketing, facilities design, site selection, new center development, and child care management systems. CCMA manage several child care centers and also own and operate HeartsHome Early Learning Center, Inc., an accredited program for infants and toddlers near the workplace.*